竹子圆

WING CHUN KUNG FU
BAMBOO RING

JOOK WAN HEUN • BAMBOO/IRON RING METHOD

Written & Illustrated by Tyler Rea

© Copyright 2013 Everything Wing Chun, LLC - All Rights reserved

Contents

General History
Details of Structure & training
The Sup yat wan "11 Ring sets"
Polarized Ring sets
• Kwan Sao wan
• Seung Gahn sao wan
• Sot Jeung
• Gum Fan Jeung wan
• Tan da wan
Un-Polarized Ring sets
• Po Pai Jeung wan
• Fong An wan
• Wan sao wan
• Look sao wan
• Biu Kiu wan
Ring Mechanics &
The 5 Fundamental Pivots
Martial Maxims
Wing Chun Terminology

© Copyright 2013 Everything Wing Chun, LLC - All Rights reserved

Dedication

Sensei Dale Wagner — Judo & Uechi Ryu
Guru Larry W. Gibson — Silat & Xingyiquan
Sifu Edmund Kwai — Wing Chun & South Mantis
Madame Tom Hoi Leong — Xingyiquan
Sifu R.L. Harris — Wing Chun & Xingyiquan
Sifu Elaine Emery — Tai Chi Chuan
Sifu Steve Cottrell — Wing Chun & Seven Star Mantis
Grand Master Brendan Lai — Seven Star Mantis
Sifu Lee Bing Choi — Wing Chun & South Mantis
Sensei Clyde Kimura — Judo & Jook Wan
Guru Carl Canliss — Balintawak, Kali Arnis
Sensei Jeff & Ann League — Aikiki Aikido
Sifu Steve Thompson — South Mantis & Bak Mei
Guru Steve Black — Kali & Silat
Guru Steve Todd — Kali & Silat
Sifu Edward Robinson III — Six Elbows Kung Fu
Sifu Mike Reyes — Six Elbows Kung Fu

Jook Wan Heun

The Jook Wan Heun or *"Bamboo Ring/Hoop"* is a training device developed in the early years of **Wing Chun Kung Fu**. Based on pictorial records and statues, Martial scholars believe that the ring was first used in religious rituals before being applied to Martial practices in temples throughout the Southern region. From temple training, the ring method was adopted by various **Secret Societies** operating within the temples, each with its own name and agenda. Once political pressure from the **Ching government** against the temples became too strong and the threat of aggression too great, many secret societies fled, taking the ring method with them. For those secret societies that were the early custodians of the Wing Chun system, the Jook Wan Heun became an ideal way to train the evolving system, but also to train beginners easily in the essential structural elements necessary for skillful Wing Chun boxing.

Groups such as the **Red Flower union, the Plum Blossom opera, the Heaven & Earth guild, the White Lotus society** and most famously the **Red Junk opera troupe** were known for cultivating the Jook Wan methods. Martial historians believe members of the nineteenth-century group called the Red Boat opera Company (aka the Red Flower union and Plum Blossom opera) used the bamboo ring as a means of training the emerging style of Wing Chun Kung Fu under the guise of a dramatic performance implement. Brightly colored and adorned on stage and wielded in dramatically choreographed routes, the ring would go unnoticed. When training on board their boats, the Red Junk members would often practice the ring method in a seated position due to conjestion on board, rough waters, or slippery decks.

In private seclusion on board the Junk the ring could be used to refine Wing Chun Boxing for a seated practitioner allowing training to go on unnoticed.

When the opera troupes disbanded, the methods of training Jook Wan techniques began to change and become more diverse. When the method moved to land the Jook Wan Ma Bo or footwork began to expend to encompass many important and diverse patterns. Pryor to leaving the Red Boats some of **the most fundamental Jook Wan Ma Bo were: Heun Bo, aka Cao Bo, Ching Cheong Ma & Hao Cheong Ma, Bik Bo, Say Ping Bo and Cheun Ma.**
Some consider the practice of the Jook Wan Heun to be the final level of solo training refinement in Wing Chun. While still others believe it to be a form of Lei sao (Loose hands) training from a Bygone era in the early days of Wing Chun before the system became so heavily codified.

Regardless of these two perspectives, the Jook Wan Heun is one of the finest and quickest methods to aquire and train the fundamentals of Wing Chun structure. Often thought of as **"Wing Chun's portable dummy"** the Jook Wan gives the practitioner the ease and fun of training anywhere, anytime, standing or seated.
This book is intended to present the fundamental training methods of the Jook Wan Heun or Bamboo Ring/Hoop of Wing Chun Kung Fu. The material and training syllabus presented are the combination of 4 of my teachers and one instructor of Judo, who became aware of this method during his childhood in hawaii.

The primary teacher and source of this material is the late **Sifu Edmund Kwai** *(Mo Kwai) 1933-1997*. His Jook Wan syllabus consists of the following:

- Sup Yat Wan
  — 11 Ring sets
- Jook Wan Da Keun
  — Bamboo ring strike fist set
- Sup Yat Wan Mor Kiu
  — 11 Link rubbing bridges

Weapons
- Lao reun Quan - Old man palm stick
- Bung Zhaa Quan - Black Moth pole
- Vagabond Opium Pipe set

The remaining material will be presented in future volumes as well as in the on-line University learning courses of *The Wing Chun University.com.* This method dovetails naturally with most Southern Chinese Kung Fu systems but Specifically renders structures most recognisable as belonging to Wing Chun. The *Jook Wan Huen* method is trained in 2 primary ring positions, one with the arms inserted parallel to each other in the ring called **Un-Polarized**. The other with the arms in pointing in opposite directions of alternating positions called **Polarized**.

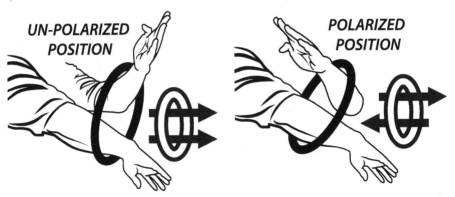

For easier reading the Jook Wan Heun or Bamboo Ring/Hoop will be abbreviated to simply the JWR throughout the rest of the book. Today the JWR's is fairly easy to find on the Internet through various online merchants *(everythingwingchun.com & shenmarti- alarts. com - ebay.com),* If you have difficulty finding one that works for you it is just as easy to make one. Most Hobby shops carry a variety of macromay hoops & crochett rings, materials may also be found at your local hardware store.

Sup yat wan

Sup yat wan or *"11 Links/ring/hoop"* are a series of 5 Polarized, & 5 Unpolarized arm positions with one outer arm position known as *Lan Wan* for a total of 11. These Ring sets may be combined with an almost limitless variety of footwork Allowing them to be trained in practically any system. Throughout the course of this book certain basic training guidelines and cheviots will be presented with each exercise to help maximize the initial stages of practise.

Sup Yat Wan 5 Polarized	Sup Yat Wan 5 Unpolarized
• Kwan Sao	• Po Pai Jeung
• Seung Gahn Sao	• Fong An Wan
• Sot Jeung	• Wan Sao
• Gum Fan Jeung	• Look Sao
• Tan Da	• Biu Kiu

Determining correct circumference

One of the first things to establish before training is to select or construct A JWR that is sized for your "Kiu" or Bridge Arm. To begin your Bridge Arm is the distance from your wrist to your elbow this Designates the surface area you use to feel and redirect the attackers pressure. Between the wrist and elbow make a non permanent mark to denote the mid line Point on the forearm Figure (A).

The circumference of your Training ring may be the full length of your forearm like the Length of Bot Jom Do Knife or it may fall to just before the Mid forearm line, Figure (B). Make certain to NEVER go below the Mid forearm line, to do so minimizes your training Circumference to the Ring and trains a point of pivot rotation That will not effect the attacker Figure (C).

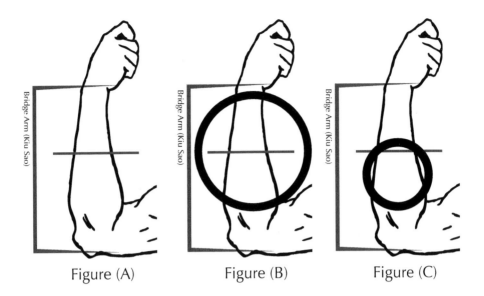

Figure (A)   Figure (B)   Figure (C)

If your JWR circumference goes below the Mid forearm line, it also makes it nearly impossible for both Bridge Arms to smoothly transision between positions with any measure of power. Training with a large Ring (one that has a circumference that goes beyond the wrist) is still acceptable and this trains the deltoids, trapezius and Lattisimus muscles to coordinate rounding the back and linking spine and stance trough pelvic lift. It was felt by my teachers that the JWR movements predated the wide spread use of a Wooden Dummy regimine. Practically all JWR exercises can be found in the Dummy sets of most Wing Chun branches, the primary ones being Kwan Sao, Seung Gahn Sao, Po Pai Jeung, Tan Da, Pak Da and Sot Jeung.

Over time as your movements become more natural, you can train each set against lit candles, so that you can begin to monitor and see how your motion affects a lit flame. You will be surprised that the more you practice it, you can naturally do what is often considered a cliched training act of putting out candles with your motion.

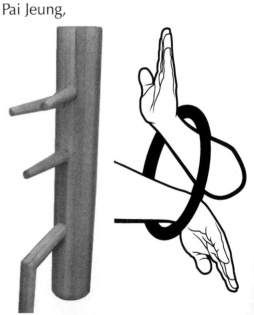

Jook Wan Huen
Lineage & Information Sources

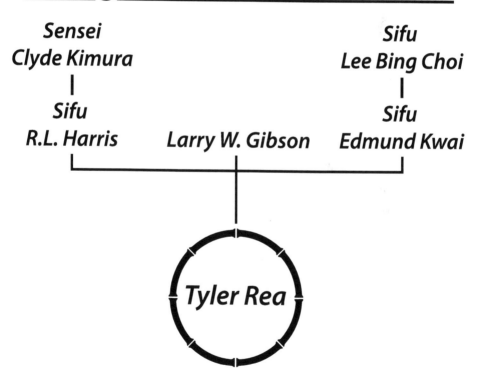

Kwan Sao wan & Seung Ghan Sao wan

Now within all the ring techniques presented, the fundamental or most crucial is called **Kwan Sao**. Known in many branches of Wing Chun this is the most fundamental of all ring positions and ring techniques. **Kwan Sao**, often called, *Noy Kwan Sao*, because you're moving force and pressure to the outside of the center line, is referenced in this way. Now, its polar opposite is called *Loy Kwan Sao*. Now **Loy Kwan Sao** is where you are deflecting force from withinto outward of the centerline.

This is also known as **Seung Ghan Sao** in some Wing Chun clans. For the sake of this book the name reference of Seung Ghan Sao will be used instead of **Loy Kwan Sao** to better deliniate the two terms. Now the detail that is important to remember about both these ring techniques as well as most of the Sup yat wan exercises is that each is a combination of pairing single arm movements together to form a single circut of structured movement. For example, Tan sao and Bong Sao are the two primary transitions in one circular circuit of motion. Whether moving in Bong Sao and then transisioning out to Tahn Sao or reversing the cycle of the circle.

With respect to both Kwan Sao and Seung Gahn sao the arms moves in a circular fashion, transitioning between Bong Sao and Tahn Sao alternating left and right sides of the center line. To reverse the circle, you're moving in from inner--what some people would call inner Ghan Sao or high-level Ghan Sao to lower Ghan or gwat sao. Also ever ring movement contains what is called Loy Chuen Sao because in all the ring motions the rotation of the bridge arm is essential for added power and ballistic rotation to your techniques.

So it is important that every arm motion not be dead or static, where you're chopping across the center line or chopping downward. There needs to be rotation as well as contraction and expansion power in your arm. Again, depending upon your branch, the names vary but the structures are essentially the same.

All ring movements contain a cycle referred to as a "Swallow and Spit" cycle, where you're spitting the power force outward and forward. The reverse is the Swallow cycle, or absorption cycle. This will be highlighted later in the unpolarized ring segments where you have **Wan Tun Sao** and **Wan Tow Sao**.

Bong, Lop, Da cycle variations from Kwan Sao.

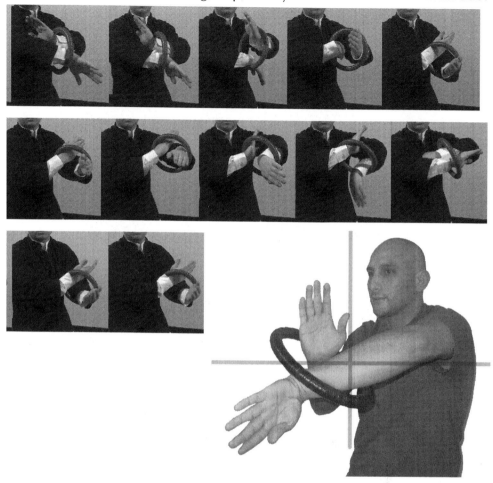

Kwan Sao cycle, 2nd section Chum Kiu with Oy seen Wai Ma step.

Please note all photo sequences flow from left to right, top to bottom.

All the ring motions are a compound movement series of two arm movement actions. With respect to the Kwan Sao, you are transitioning a Tahn and Bong motion on both sides of the body with both arms, but each being polarized in opposite references of timing. For example, the transition of Dai Bong Sao to Tan here polarizes and reverses itself. This is again crucial to understanding how the hands cycle too defend you.

The second, being Loy Chun Sao and the lower Gwat or Ghan Sao formin the structural foundation of **Seung Ghan sao**. Think of **Kwan Sao & Seung Ghan sao** as two parents, and they create the entire variation and proliferation of all Jook wan ring techniques as thier children.

When practicing **Seung Ghan Sao** aka, *(Loy Kwan Sao)* it's important to know that within the transition of the movement, the lower hand may perform a Jik Choi or straight punch. When you transition and deal with an attacker who comes at you with two hands and you deflect him off the center line, the lower hand is the first striking hand, because it is both more difficult to defend and more difficult to see within the scope of the technique because it hides under the elbow. The **Seung Gahn Sao** movement is generaly found in the Biu Jee form and wooden dummy set of most Wing Chun branches. **Seung Ghan Sao** is most often translated as double "cultivating" hands. It is more accurately described as double cleaving hands, the way a plow cleaves the soil. This description highlights the importance of **Seung Ghan Sao** to displace the attackers movement while moving forward. **Seung Ghan Sao** on a basic level is the reversed movement of Kwan Sao and, as such, the low Gahn Sao hand has elements of Gwat Sao.

Many ancient Chinese boxing manuals say that the fist that hides under the elbow is the one that carries Death's seal. So when you apply the motion of Loy Kwan Sao or Seung Ghan Sao, be aware that you have a Jik Choi at your disposal within the transition. This also replicates the structural transitions of Sot Geung, the Killing Palms motion. Again you'll see that many of these movements are variations on a theme but a very important theme that runs throughout the whole course of the structured movements of the Jook Wan.

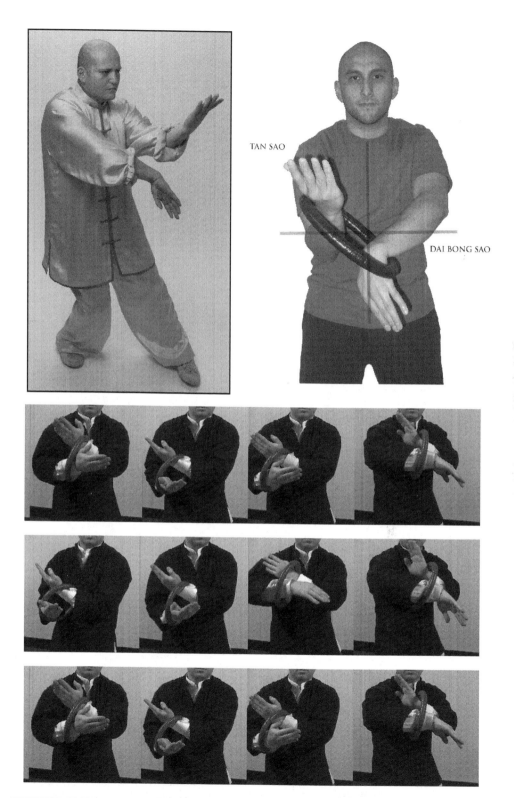

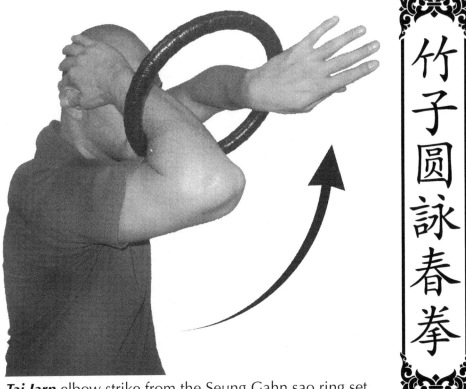

Tai Jarn elbow strike from the Seung Gahn sao ring set.

Kwan Sao may be linked with many types of footwork, but the techniques discussed here require the use of • Ching Cheong Ma, (Forward Brace horse) • Hao Cheong Ma, (Rear Brace horse) • Som Kwak Ma, (Triangle horse) • Chuen Ma, (Turning horse) & Bik Ma (Jamming horse).

When practising Kwan Sao with the JWR & the Cheun Ma stance turn make sure you do not pivot beyond a rotation angle of 45 degrees from the centerline. This keeps the development of power & pressure within The structure range of the Jo Hao Ma (Left Mid horse) & Yao Hao Ma (Right Mid horse) positions, drilling power down the centerline over time.

45° Angle Boundary

45° An Bound

Seung Ghan Sao cycle with Cheun Ma turning horse.

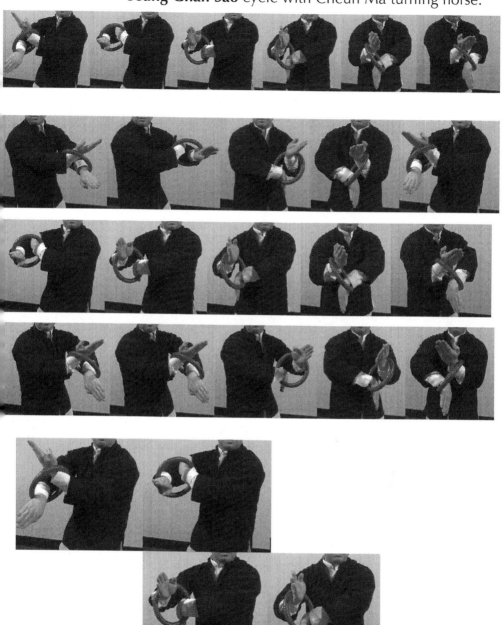
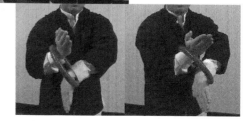

Sot Jeung wan

Now within the Sup Yat Wan, there is one palm technique, one ring technique, know as **Sot Geung**, literally means *killing palms*. My teacher, Edmund Kwai, referred to it as the ***Devil Gate Palm or Devil Guardian Palm*** simply because Sot Geung is a transitional technique and transitional attack position that can be applied between all of the ring techniques. It is like the crossroads or the intersection point of all of the techniques. For example, when posing Kwan Sao, immediately you can deflect and move into the Sot Geung technique. Sot Geung is considered a variation of Po Pai Jeung, but again out of the polarized ring position.

Sot Jeung, without the ring, is composed of a lower **Dai Wong Jeung**, also know as **Chang Dai Jeung**, (lower spade hand) and a Fak Sao, sometimes called Pai Sao or hacking arm. This motion can be used with the Phoenix Eye puch, the Ger Nah Choi (Ginger fist punch) as well It can be used with any specialty hand fist that you wish to use within it.

Sot Jeung, within the unpolarized ring position is considered a much simpler expression of the technique then when the hands are in the Polarized ring position and resembles the butterfly palm or Po Pai Jeung technique. Strike attacks naturaly flow from the left and right sides ***(Jo Hao Ma, Yao Hao Ma positions)***, defending left and right gates.

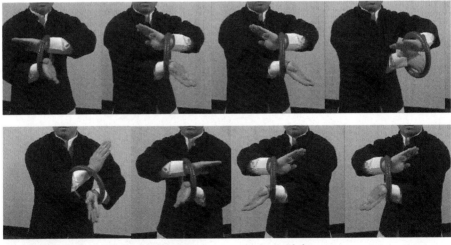

Sot Jeung wan cycle with Cheun Ma turning horse.

Gum Fan Jeung wan

Gum Fan Jeung is a motion sequence which replicates many motions that utilize the Tan Sao portion of the Kwan Sao ring set to perform backhand line attacks. Within some schools of Wing Chun, backhand line attacks are frowned upon and they fall under a terminology category called **Gwa Choi,** which means "Hanging Punch." Sometimes called **Fan Cup Choi** or "Overturning punch" and then within some schools of Southern Mantis, **Gao Choi**, or "Thunder punch."

But regardless of the branch that one is familiar with, out of the Kwan Sao motion, the Fan Gum Jeung is this sequence, where you're taking the upper Tan hand and it is transitioning to perform an Gum or pinning motion, past the bridge arm, near the elbow, wiping and surpressing while the Bong Sao hand transitions upward into the Tan kiu position, Tan kiu being roughly translated as "dispersing/spread out bridge" or "spring bridge" position.

In this instance, we're using it as a backhand line attack. This is very crucial and often overlooked because within the scope of an actual fight, sucessful techniques boil down to those that at their heart are very gross motor movements. Therefore it's essential that your line of attack intersect all possible lines of attack that come at you.

When attacked, the angle and type of attack is unknown. It's essential that your motion intersect all possible angles along the centerline. Just as a fisherman when fishing uses a net to fish a large area within the body of water, you don't want to fish within the space of a bucket or dinner plate. You want to cast a broad net so that you can catch as much as possible, so too with an attacker.

When they launch an attack at you you want to intersect their motion from here and you want to do so with a movement that exemplifies a very powerful outer circular circumference. All the bridge arm positions within the Jook wan training, at their core are meant to replicate the outer circumference of a circle and most importantly of a sphere. We take the structural template of the ring from here and imagine that it is much larger, almost the size of a hula hoop, that we are embracing from here.

You want your arm structure from shoulder to wrist to aproximate one third of a sphere or a circle so that you have roughly 135 degree bend to your arm so the structural integrity is intact and with the use of what is called **Jiang Dai Lik** or "elbow sinking power" you want that circumference to be cast out at the attacker so that you intersect their force and metaphorically, just like being put under the wheels of a bus, you want that force to rip and tear them down to the ground and go forward so that you can attack them.

Within the scope of **Fan Gum Jeung**, take your Bong Sao hand, press downward, making certain that you stay within the circumference of the ring. Refrain from breaking contact with the ring. The ring again is to articulate and guide your arms within the circular motion. When you do so, try to refrain from training it quickly, again, you want every part of the body to participate in this motion sequence. You don't want one part of the body to become prematurely excited or prompted to move and break its sequence with all the other sections of the body. Make certain that you train movements slowly and smoothly, staying within the corrective structure of the ring/hoop, so that the timing of the hands and the rotation, "the Cheun ging", is correct and accurate. Later, once this becomes natural, you can train this motion against lit candles, so that you can begin to monitor and see how your motion affects a lit flame.

Fan Gum Jeung wan cycle with Cheun Ma turning horse.

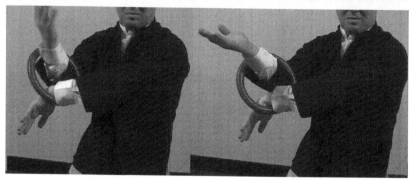

Please note all photo sequences flow from left to right, top to bottom.

Tan Da wan

The fundamental techniques of **Tan Da** can also be found within the Jook Wan syllabus. It is trained in two primary ways. The first of which is with the hands inserted in position two of unpolarized where one hand touches the shoulder of the opposite side, Initiates Tan Sao and a Jik choi straight punch. Then the ring transitions where you touch the opposite side shoulder, transition and repeat Tahn Da. This is one way in which the sequence is practiced, often with Cheun Ma footwork or Oy and Noy Seem Wai footwork. It is fairly basic, effective and I present it here because you will see it amongst other clans' representation of the Jook Wan. It is also very effective when training with a much larger hoop so that you can traverse through the four gates much easier with the ring, applying the **Tahn Da** technique. The one that I'd like to focus on here is in the polarized position, just like within Kwan Sao, we have the child of Kwan Sao, this variation of Tan Da, where the hand comes up and you punch forward in this fashion.

Where the **Tan sao** hand is obliquely referenced on the centerline with the Jik Choi below. Again, they are staggered on the centerline, allowing you to turn and cycle between the left and right side horse stances with the Tahn Da technique, displacing the attack off the centerline in a very aggressive wedge-like fashion, which will be shown in the applications, But again this replicates in some respects the important details of why some systems like White Eyebrow Boxing have their salute contrived the way they do.

Through this ring set, of **Tan Da** you can begin to immediately experience and express the important body mechanics of what are called the **four energies (Say Ging): float, sink, swallow, and spit** to that your ring motion will have that contract and expand quality necessary to the discharge power in multiple directions.

When using it against an attacker's punching arm, you're using your **Tan Da** to displace that arm and punch them in the flank. Refrain if you can from heading for the face. It's a somewhat odd habit in

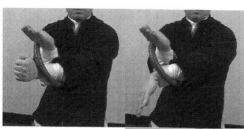

Tan Da wan cycle with Cheun Ma turning horse.

Tan Da wan cycle with Cheun Ma turning horse.

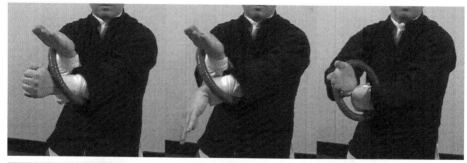

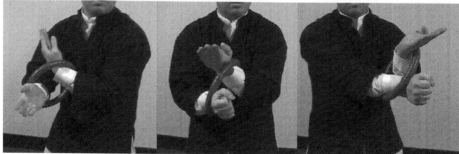

Please note all photo sequences flow from left to right, top to bottom.

America especially that applications reference punching a person in the face and head. Whereas there's a time for all applications in training, try to avoid that for the simple respect that the human mouth is a very bacteria laden environment. The most bacteria laden environment on the entire human body.

As such its important in a day and age when HIV, AIDS, and hepatitis are commonplace that you not punch an attacker in the mouth. You are virtually guarantied to get your hand broken, but if you cut your hands on their teeth, you will receive a very, very nasty wound that will become infected and cause you some severe problems. So again, avoid the mouth for the sake of your own personal hygiene and safety. In a more longterm way, refrain from punching a person straight in the face.

Please know I am not advocating a particular act of violence, but when you have to use your self-defense techniques, try to reference your palm for the face, that way you don't break your hand. Now from the neck down, targets are ideal for a closed fist, so you don't break your hand. So in respect to the **Tan Da** technique, make sure you're aiming for any abdominal target below the shoulder, whether it's centerline referenced or flank referenced near an attacker's lattisimus dorsals doesn't matter. Just make sure you reference the attack low.

Other details about **Tan Da** that are important to note are that the hand, the punching hand here, will rotate along the lower portion of the ring's circumference. Again, this pressure triggers the rest of the hoop to cue the upper hand so that you're receiving tactile sensitivity information to both hands through the hoop and ring that relates reciprocally to rotational power.

So that as you're hitting from here the punching hand as you're rotating through so that it then traverses downward along the opposite shoulder and hip region, upward almost through the arm pit. If you can see the hand as it descends through the armpit region it's passing through your carotid zone around your neck.

This is another wonderful facet of the ring training and it is that your arms are treated like bone shields and these bone shields traverse bleeding zones around the body providing back-up protection.

Here with **Tan Da** the lower hand is dropping downward to fall within the region of my femoral artery near the pelvis. So we have carotid, brachial, femoral near the pelvis. From here, the hand descends, striking out, striking out, drops down, ascends again to the neck, punching from here. So that you have built in form of defense as your hands are transitioning and cycling to reload this attack.

Another aspect of what's sometimes called **Lao Ging** or "leaking force' is that when the arm is twisting as I just pointed out and sinking down, this hand is covering so that the hands are looping in a way that if you receive too much force or presure in your bridge arms, your hands can turn and spring forward in almost exactly the same way as the Siu Nim Tao form when people perform their double Ghan Sao hand and their lower hand will spring up to defend against trapping actions. That same mechanic is built into this ring set.

So to the best of your ability practice the **Tan Da** ring technique with this in mind. Train it slowly and smoothly. Try not to get frustrated that the ring will force and confine your hands to stay within the boudaries of your shoulders so that you don't depart beyond at 45 degree angle of line facing.

Within Jook Wan training there are two primary positions with which to use the ring. The first, ***position one***, is called **Polarized**, where both hands are inserted within the ring in opposite directions. The second, ***position two*** is called **Unpolarized**. It is where both bridge arms face the same direction, positioned parallel to each other within the ring.

Po Pai Jeung

Po Pai Jeung means "Butterfly Palms" and is practiced in ring Position 2 *(Un-Polarized)*. Begin with both hands inserted parallel two each other in the ring. If standing with the right leg forward, make sure the left hand covers on top of the right hand. This makes sure that the right hand is deployed first and forward, Allowing it to hook outward in the Pao Jeung position. As with all the JWR sets, each movement of the right or left arm is designed to serve as back-up for the other at all times. This aspect is most evident in the Po Pai Jeung set but is a function of all.

The standard Po Pai Jeung cycle found in most Wing Chun clans **Wooden Dummy** set (The Mook Yan Jong) and introduces the student to the importance of palm applications in the system. **Po Pai Jeung** is a movement that expresses some of the highest skills of sticking and bridge arm adhesion. **Po Pai Jeung** is Designed to facilitate fast and flowing trapping actions that bind the attackers bridge arm as well as skeletal fame when coupled with the jamming attributes of the Wing Chun stance. **Po Pai Jeung** comprises a majority of the palm applications within the Wooden dummy set, within some Non-Yip Man branches over 60% of the set is devoted to **Po Pai Jeung.** This level of dual palm training is meant to enhance the coordinated use of the open hand to deliver greater power to zones in and around the rib cage. **Po Pai Jeung** is also meant to prepare the student for the use of double weapons, in most branches the Double knives or **Bot jom do** training stage to come.

Po Pai jeung applications highlight the importance of safe non radial artery contact points when dealing with a weapon.

Po Pai Jeung cycle with Centeral pivot rotation between wrists.

Po Pai Jeung cycle with Toe Ma horse.

Po Pai Jeung cycle with Toe Ma horse.

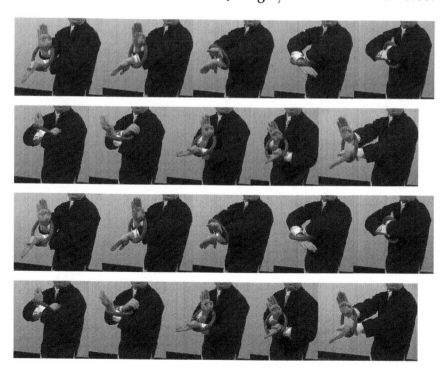

Fong An Wan

The **Fong An Wan** set develops center point & circumference pivot rotation to alternate the application of the Fong An Choi (Phoenix Eye punch) and the Wu Sao guard. The action of forward pressure in the punch may also be used in a Jum Kiu (Sinking Bridge) fashion to suppress the attackers arm and then counter strike.

The method of central pivot rotation is of extreme importance when trying to dissolve the aggressive pressure of an edged weapon attack. The alternating and reciprocal application of non-radial contact points is a safety detail of great benefit in moments when a sudden knife attack requires an instant deflection that also serves as a strike. The preferred striking surface in the Fong an wan aside from the Phoenix eye punch itself is the inner forearm bone or Ulna bone and heal of the fist or Bien Choi strike.

The **Phoenix Eye Fist,** called in Cantonese **Feng An Choi** or in Mandarin **Foeng Yung Chueh.** There are Several facets of this compact and close-quarter striking method that make it an effective favorite strike in kung fu. The fist, which is formed by sequentially closing the fingers into a fist beginning with the little finger, on up to the middle, and then folding the index finger back upon the support of the thumb.

The **Phoenix Eye Fist** affords the user several unique options in the choice of striking surfaces. (1) Striking with the frontal face of the index finger. (2) Striking with the back face of the index finger. (3) Striking with the frontal face of the fist. (4) Striking with the nail or knuckle of the thumb. Gouging the eye is the easiest with the thumb, the strongest digit. (5) The Whip punch surface known as Bien Choi and Pek Choi, a Hammer fist strike, which falls under the umbrella of Gao Choi. (6) The Back hand punch surface known as Gwa Choi and Bung Choi, which also falls under the umbrella of Gao Choi.

It is important to note that one should refrain from striking with the very tip of the **Phoenix Eye Fist.** Initially, this sounds unavoidable and incorrect, but striking with the tip of the fist is very hard on the joint. Prior to the use of gloves in boxing, in the days of bare-knuckle matches, both fighters' hands were usually broken (to a greater or lesser extent) by the second or third round. *It is important* to

Fong An wan cycle with Toe Ma horse.

strike with the bone support inherent in the position of the knuckle fold because this affords the best structural support possible to the most fragile of the bones. Whether training with the aid of Dit Da medicine or not, one should use care in all Martial practices.

Striking paper or a piece of cardboard is by far the safest and naturally the cheapest method for training to be accurate with the Phoenix Eye strike. Apply various configurations of dots to the **Paper/Cardboard/Foamcore board** and practice striking without disturbing or tearing the whole target, striving to pierce with a small point. An excellent and equally affordable target is a shower curtain.

The eye of the phoenix is a quick strike with the knuckle of the index finger. This is an extremely effective technique when applied to pressure points and delicate areas of the body such as the throat, temple, and armpits also on sensitive exposed area such as the ribs, solar plexus and kidneys. This strike is effective because all the momentum and striking power is focused in a small area of a single point.

Details to be aware of:
First — Do so compromises the structural integrity of the punch by executing it from a chambered hip position. Chambered hip deployment makes targeting with the punch very, very difficult and adds excessive time to the punch.

Second — Keep the bridge arms in front of the body with the elbows down, being stabilized by gravity *(through relaxed trapezius and deltoid muscles)* and manifest what the Chinese call **Jang Dai Lik** *(Elbow sinking power)*. The punch should first be executed from a distance of no longer than 12 inches *(from start to finish)* and then over time cover a shorter and shorter distance to the target, training down to an inch or less.

Third — This punch should NOT be executed in conjunction with long or wide bridging steps, simply because this is a close-quarter strike and is meant to be used with footwork that makes adjustments within inches of the attacker. It is advisable not to strike a heavy bag, with a Phoenix eye fist or to do so on a Wooden Dummy for obvious reasons.

THE PHOENIX EYE PUNCH

Wan Sao

(Linked or Cyclic Hands) **Wan Sao** uses the structures of Bong Sao & Tan Sao in Three Basic Planes of movement to develop greater power and structure with Yin & Yang power arcs of pressure.
The Five Basic Planes of movement are:
- Vertical linear rising Tan or Bong transition.
- Horizontal linear Tan or Bong transition.
- Circular Tan to Bong transition.
- Swallowing Tan to Bong transition (Wan tun sao)
- Spitting Tan to Bong transition (Wan toe sao)

Wan Sao uniquely focuses on the unification of planes of bridge arm movement with that of the body's core torso mass. This important ring set lays the foundation for the application of Duan ging (short/inch power) much sought after in the martial arts.

To the right a Dai Kwai jarng Elbow strike application from Wan sao.

Horizontal Wong Wan sao cycle with Cheun Ma.
with Seung Dai Bong sao

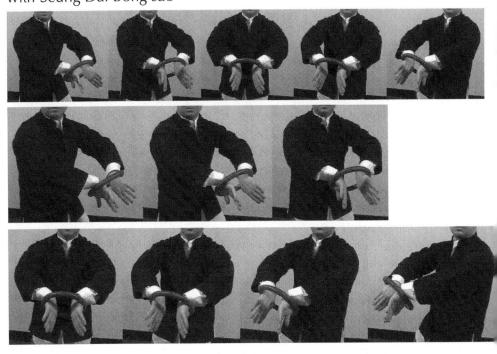

Horizontal Wong Wan sao cycle with Cheun Ma.
with Seung Chung Tan sao

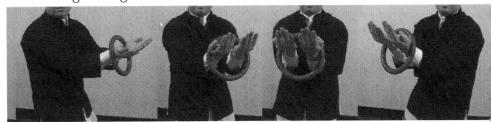

Vertical rising Tai Wan sao cycle with Cheun Ma.
from Seung Dai Bong sao to Seung Chung Tan sao

Biu Kiu

The "Thrusting Bridge" **Biu Kiu** is a ring set that focuses heavily on the deployment of **Cheong kiu ging** *(Long braced bridge power)*. Biu Kiu contains many bridge arm methods generally seen in systems like **White Eyebrow (Bak Mei) & South Mantis**, however the Jook wan imposes the Sao fot calibration of the **Five pivots** too

When practicing the movements make sure the tips of your fingers do not exceed the height of your eyebrows, nor should they fall below the solar plexus. The **Biu Kiu** exercise should have the following elements:

First - the Forearms need to maintain a position as parallel as possible to the ground.

Second - Forearm rotation should be evident throughout the extension of the movement.

Third - Train this movement **SLOWLY!**

Presented in the following pages are the basic training details of the Iron roller/ Iron pole training devise to aid in the cultivation of Wing Chun Cheong kiu ging bridge arms skills. The key mental focus is on unyielding forward penetration driven from the spine rooted through the stance.

Biu Kiu wan cycle with Toe Ma applying Seung Biu kiu

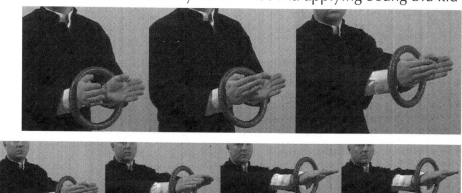

The Iron Ruler, or Rolling Pole

This simple and remarkable training device is normally found within the southern boxing traditions, but was first introduced to me through Yiquan.

This device is generally made for a student by the instructor but an item as simple as a Stick, Staff or pole may be substituted. In the past a Rolling Pole was made of bamboo or a hollowed section of wood, filled with small rocks, sand or water for resistance.

To construct a modern version acquire a section of PVC pipe as long as your arm and no thinner in circumference than 3 fingers, unless your using a staff.

Cap and secure with adhesive one end of the PVC pipe and then fill only half way with small stones, sand or copper/zinc BB's. Cap and secure with adhesive the other end of the PVC pipe and let rest until adhesive has set.

Rolling Pole details..

Illustration right is a cut away showing the resistance material within. The purpose of a resistance material such as small stones, sand or copper/zinc BB's or water is not only to add an element of interactivity but to fine tune small muscle movements generally supressed my major muscle movements.

Rolling Pole Exercise 1 - Forward penetrating extension:

Begin standing in a stance slightly wider than shoulder width. Place the Roller pole evenly balanced across your forearms. The position of your palms throughout the whole of exercise one is with the palms facing each other as if holding a loaf of bread between them.

Begin by slowly and smoothly extending your arms forward so that the roller contours the length of your forearms from wrist to elbow bend. As you extend your arms forward they will rise slightly, the main detail is to keep the forearms as parallel as possible to the ground, so that the interaction of Roller pole and extending bridge arms is a smooth and seamless dovetail of movement. The Mind Intent is on the smooth forward extension of the arms supported by the back and elbows converging near the center line plane. Breathing should be calm and natural as you focus your awareness on the expansion and contraction of the bodys frame during the movement.

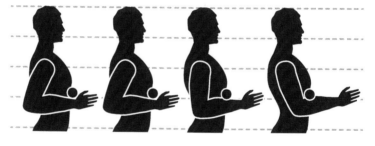

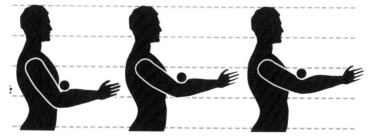

Roller pole Exercise 1 Movement Sequence

Rolling Pole Exercise 2 - Rise and Fall arm extension:

Begin as in exercise 1, place the Roller pole evenly balanced across your forearms. The position of your palms throughout the whole of exercise two is with the palms facing down as if holding a cup of hot coffee trying not to spill.

Begin by slowly and smoothly extending your arms forward as they rise slightly focus and point with the wrists as the palms flex slightly downward. Again the main detail is to keep the forearms as parallel as possible to the ground, as the Roller pole evenly moves over the forearms.

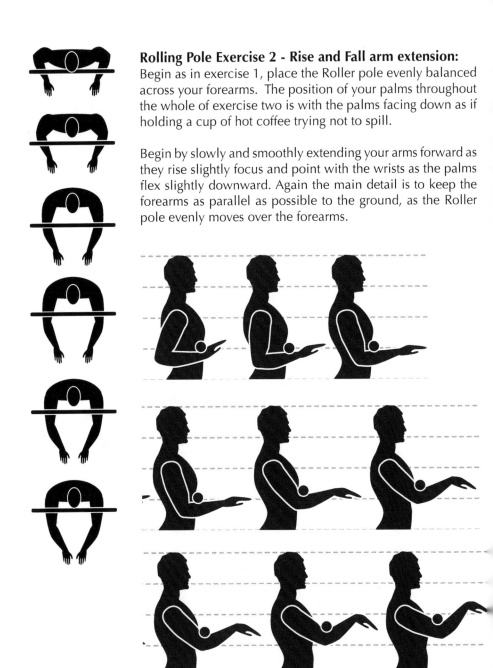

Roller pole Exercise 2 Movement Sequence

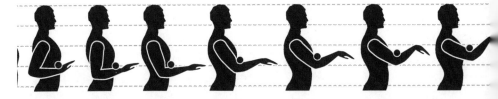

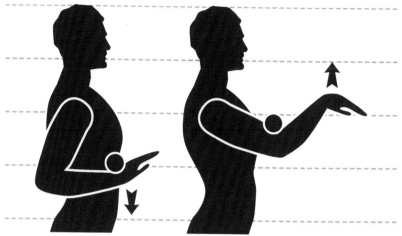

Rolling Pole Exercise 2 continued:

The focus should be on the rhythmic cycle of rise and fall of the hands and wrists in contrast to the movement of the Roller pole as it moves in the opposite direction heightening an awareness of contradictory forces.

This movement is known in Yiquan as "Turtle emerges from the Sea" cycle and over time may be practiced with the appropriate footwork from that exercise. However far more important is the initiation of slight slow movement that acts on the Roller pole in small increments to maintain a flow of movement that is not abrupt.

Persistent practice of these exercises refines and heightens an awareness of the spacial boundaries of the "4 corners". The "4 corners" represent the boundary areas of the shoulders and hips forming a box that extends out in 3 dimensional space. It is this area that your arms must dominate in a fight not exceeding the height of the eyebrows or falling below the waist.

Rolling Pole Exercise 3 - Forward Ballistic Rotation:

Begin as in exercises 1 & 2 with Roller pole across the forearms. Your hands should be palm up not exceeding the width of your shoulders. Begin by slowly and smoothly extending your arms forward, transitioning the palms to a position where each palm faces each other and fingers point forward as in exercise 1. Your movement should continue uninterrupted in extension with the palms ending palm down.

With this exercise you should become aware of artificial point of rotation axis extending from your shoulder out too and outside of your palms. Your arms should orbit around this pivot axis contouring it as if it were a physical object like a tapered nose cone under your arm pointing outward.

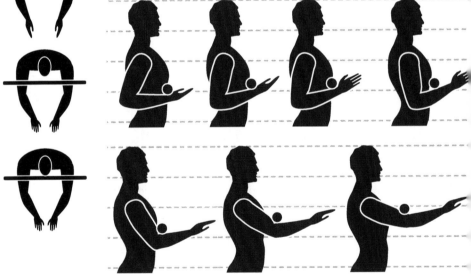

Roller pole Exercise 3 Movement Sequence

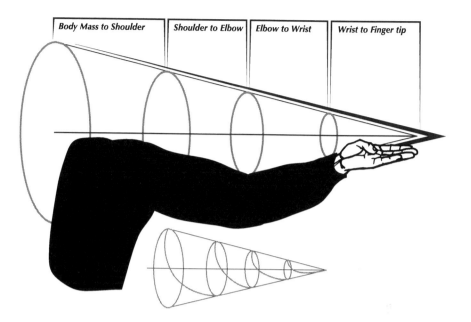

Rolling Pole details..

Persistent practise with the Roller will develop a Vorticular forward Coiling power in your bridge arm when it is extended. As indicated above each segment of the arm expresses a unique diameter of Axial rotation like the various gear segments of a bike. These Axial rotation segments allow the user to apply greater and greater levels of displacment power that bores through the attacker. When all Axial rotation segments plus body mass are discharged together at one moment bursting inch power is released, like that of a drilling donino chain that tears through the attackers structure. As indicated below each segment of the arm expresses a unique wieght displacement ratio as well. Each of these weight segments especially the elbow and Body mass discharge great power when united with gavities pull through relaxed Sung body structure.

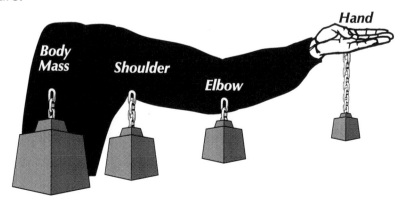

Look Sao
Look sao or "Rolling hands" is just as it's name suggests, how- ever this simple and overlooked exercise contains many fine points. While developing the practitioners ability to drill vorticular power down the centerline Look sao also reinforces the 135 degree deflection angle of the bridge arm, in conjunction with the transition between Bong sao & Tan sao crucial to sticking hands practise when not with a partner.

Seung Lan Sao with Cheun Ma
This exercise provides a way to train the stance pivot of Wing Chun while holding the static posture of a Double Lan Sao variation.
The structural detail or a relaxed trapezius muscle and rooted sunken elbows are keys too uniting the backs spine power to the arms and deploying that power beyond the body.

The Devils Detail
Probably the single most important reason to train with the JWR has to due with point of rotation. In nature any display of power on a grand scale has to due with Rotation power. (Windmills, Tornados, Whirlpools, Planetary rotation and Planetary orbit, Super nova collapses or expansion etc.) When using the JWR the hands, and specifically the wrists are in constant contact with the inner circumference of the Ring, this causes the arms to rotate around an artificial pivot point.

First: when the arms move in this way orbiting around this artificial pivot point they have greater mass than they would if the axis of rotation ran through the ulna & radial bone area. (As well as greater deflection surface area.)
Second: through the rise and fall of the elbow, the arms generate greater power through the second most important element (the first being the change in pivot), Enhanced expansion and contraction of the arms ability to generate Power.

This is further amplified through the integrated use of the spine (lifting of pelvis & rounding of the backs scapula), this and adding the bodies mass (through the stance rotation) more than potentially doubles the power produced. (Rare instances Tripling Power)
Seung Kuen Naturally flows out of Kwan Sao and Po Pai Jeung.

Seung Lan Sao with cycle with Cheun Ma.

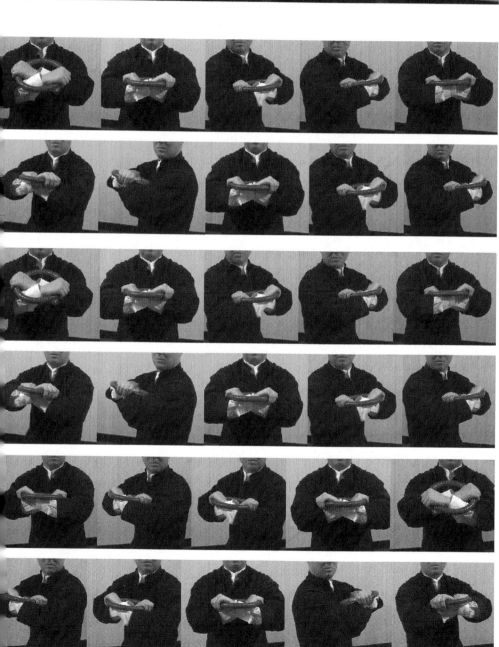

Dragon Prawn or ***"Shrimp Back mechanics"*** One element of JWR training that can be cultivated that is very important to advanced power generation is Dragon Prawn or Shrimp Back.
Through the pelvic lift tilt you have been practising in conjunction with an awareness of your breathing (Inhale you Rise, Exhale you Sink) you may begin to pulse your pressure and force up through your stance and out to the hands.
Dragon Prawn or Shrimp Back is so named due to the appearance of the practitioners back looking like a Shrimp. This appearance should be momentary at the point of power discharge, and results from the spines shape being transformed from an "S" shape to that of a "C" thus replicating the structure of the oldest Kinetic spring or Bow.

Fan Gwan Jong or "Spring Pole Dummy"
An invaluable training aid that can be built dirt cheep is the Spring Pole Dummy. Made to replicate the vertical structure and spring tension resistance of Bamboo a Spring Pole Dummy provides a fantastic supplement to 2 person training that can greatly develop power, sticking coordination. Simply attach an Eye bolt to the ends of a wooden pole, next attach three additional eye bolts, (2 at the bottom of a door frame and one to the ceiling) attach short bungee cords to the ends to link the tension and practise any of the exercises presented here to add another dimension to your Martial training.

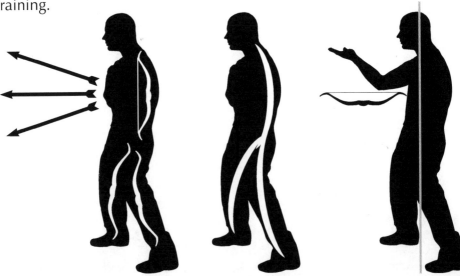

© Copyright 2013 Everything Wing Chun, LLC - All Rights reserved

Ma Gung & Bo Fot Stance & Stepping

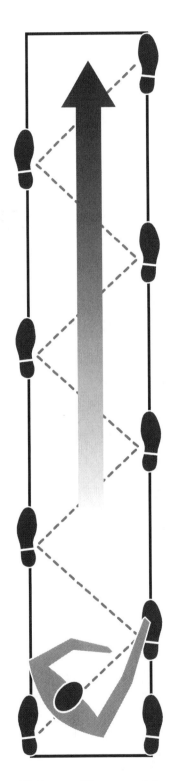

Oy Seen Wai Toe Ma
Left

Oy Seen Wai Toe Ma
Right

Ching Chong Ma

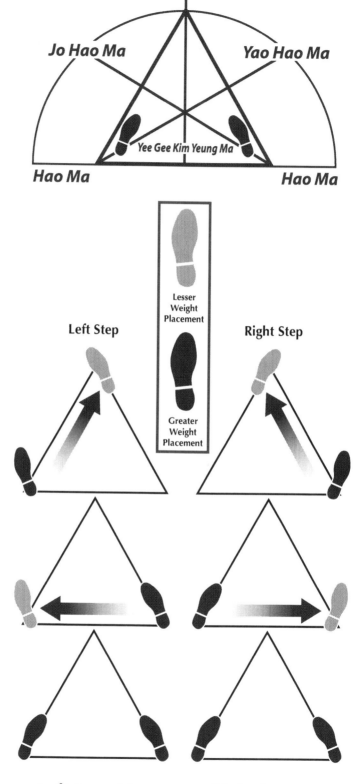

Say Ging — 4 Energies

The Four Energies of, Tun To Fau Chum means **Float, Sink, Swallow and Spit.** The first one is to apply "tun to" to body shape. So "tun to" can also be translated by shrinking and stretching. The second way is to consider only the air we breath. "Tun to" is then related to a breathing pattern (breathe in; breathe out, stop breath and press air down to tighten the abdomen.). "Tun to" is then translated by inhale and exhale. In both body shape and breathing, these concepts deal with generating power in a specific way. For Kung fu practitioners, the bottom line is not to acquire force but to acquire power. That is the reason why **Tun to Fau Chum is considered as the core of kung fu**. Acquiring explosive power in kung fu leads to work on tendons. The muscles have to be softened, hardened, shrunk and stretched. The spinal column is used in such a way that the back of a practitioner looks hunched. The ribs also seem to contribute to the power generation. Tun to fau chum is the feature which make people say that a system is an internal style.

The main Attacking power is **Geng Ging, The "Scared Power" Or "Shock Power.** This concept is almost the trademark of kung fu. But there are two ways to describe it. The first one is to bring out a power which is understood as a rapid contraction of the muscle. It is the same power that people get when suddenly scared. The second way is to see gang ging is the power which shakes up the opponent as if he gets scared or shocked. For attack, the Actions of the hands are tight and close, elbows need to be sunk, and shoulders to be loose. The focus of the long hand action and short hand action is short or even none. Defined as **Say noi biu ging**, literally the four internally-supported expulsive forces, the four characteristics are tan, tou, fau, and chum. Within this context, the internal aspect is addressed by the structurally integrated mechanics of look ging. The issuing force assumes a directional charge derived from the compressing and releasing dynamics of the waist, core muscles, and back.

Tun, literally meaning to swallow, redirects an opponent's incoming force into the ground. In essence, the practitioner grounds the energy of an attack with this action. **Tou,** or to spit, corresponds to an outward release of force away from the body. Typically, tun complements tou as a kinetic pair. **Fou,** to float, is an uprooting force that disrupts and displaces the opponent's foundation. This

SAY GING
(4 ENERGIES)

漂 (FOU)	沉 (CHUM)	啍 (TUN)	吐 (TOU)
Float	**Sink**	**Swallow**	**Spit**
Rise	Fall	Expand	Contract
Up	Down	Pull	Push
Ascend	Descend	Backward	Forward
Disconnect	Root	Absorb	Expel
Buoyant	Firm	Enter Void	Leave Void
Flex out	Flex in	Rotate in	Rotate out
Scatter	Solidify	Converge	Separate
Polarize	Unify	Charge	Discharge

Fou - *Float*   **Chum** - *Sink*   **Tun** - *Swallow*   **Tou** - *Spit*

© Copyright 2013 Everything Wing Chun, LLC - All Rights reserved

enables the practitioner to take advantage of the adversary's vulnerable state. On the other hand, **Chum,** a sinking action, bears weight onto the opponent in a suppressing manner. Again, this provides the practitioner the opportunity to capitalize on the adversary's submissive state.

The concepts of **Tan, Tou, Fau, Cham** are found in many Southern Chinese martial arts and their combative interpretation can range from isolated to integrated actions. Some styles translate this formula as an expression of the extremities such as hand techniques swallowing, releasing, raising, or pressuring the limbs of an opponent's attacks. Others view this concept as one arising from a holistic source based upon the principles of connected and coordinated movements reinforcing techniques.

The Structure Formula for Power in Chinese boxing

If we look at the body's ability to produce power for striking, we can see that it is very important to access the body's full mass. The body has three parts that can be used as kinetic springs—the legs, arms, and spine. In comparison to the legs and arms, the torso or spine contains the greatest amount of mass.

In practically the same way a medieval catapult or French trebuchet utilizes a downward, falling counterweight to generate its ballistic power, so too does this boxing method. It is through the first two polarized energy extremes of float and sink that this is accomplished.

Once the spring power systems of the stance (legs) and torso (spine) are linked through the rolled forward pelvic lift, it is time to unlock the power within the scapula gate. The image of a gate expresses an open and closed polarity. Similarly, the compound lever action of the scapula, trapezius, and shoulder create an open and closed opposition. This is acomplished within the two primary polarized states of **Retraction & Protraction.** This very critical detail allows the practitioner to access the body's torso mass and deploy the resulting power in the six major ging directions. Through the act of rounding the back (Hom Hon and Tan Hang) and swallowing the chest, the scapula bones become the source of and deployment point for the arms' striking power.

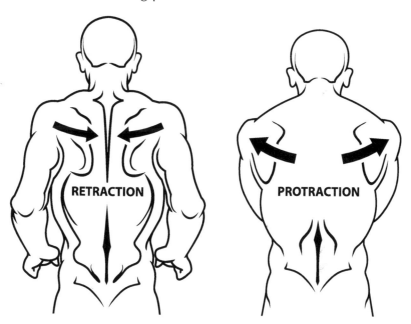

This action and detail of movement allows the practitioner **FIRST** to strike without the retraction of the arms that commonly occurs in other systems. It is a common practice in most systems to retract and withdraw the striking arm to wind up a punch. This winding-up motion consumes time you do not have, opens vulnerable space, and violates the core principle of "no retraction."

SECOND attacking motions are therefore no longer isolated strictly to movements initiated by the forearm, which would break the chain of power discharge.

THIRD, any rebound contact force from the attacker can be channeled and dissipated from the bridge arm contact through the spine,

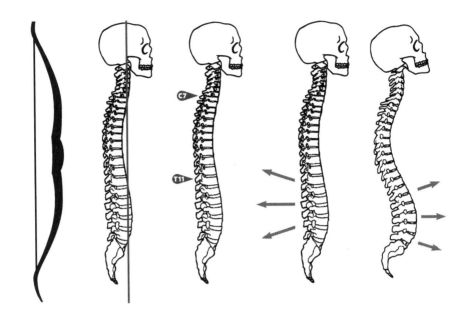

down the legs to the ground, away from the practitioner.
Visualize for a moment the cross-bracing found in a child's kite. Imagine a vertical axis (the spine) and a horizontal bracing axis that connects the shoulders, intersecting the vertical spine axis at the cervical vertebra C7.

Now, just as with the kite, visualize a line, a string, a centerline plane extending from your center to the attacker. The next visualization will sound counterintuitive, but please keep an open mind. Imagine the above-mentioned cross-bracing structure in your body, facing the attacker squarely and contracting in a way that forces the intersection point of the two perpendicular lines out the back.

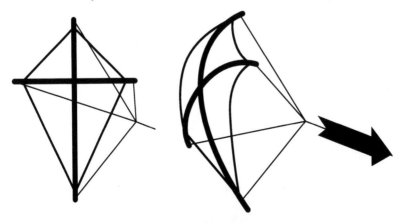

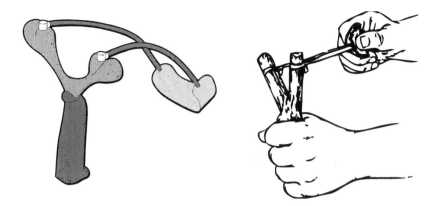

When applied, this is the act of rounding the back that extends forward and inward the ends of the cross-bracing structure, which would discharge power down the centerline plane towards an attacker. If this is hard to imagine, picture the torso as the pocket of a slingshot, with the center of the pocket being at the point between the shoulder blades.

When you round the back, it is like drawing back a slingshot, creating tension that can be released forward in an explosive manner. The force projected by the spinal kinetic spring is like the stone released from the slingshot.

This is the development of Power through gravitys partnership. Since the beginning of our lives we as human beings have been acutely aware of the presence of gravity and since our early development as children learning to crawl, to stand and then finally to walk, gravity has exerted a constant influence on our bodies. As a result we have each learned naturally to move to a great or lesser degree with gravity and to balance ourselves against it's influence, in doing so over the years we also develop an inherent accumulation of body tension. This tension is the result of our bodies constant attempt at structural self-correction.

(FOU)
FLOAT

(CHUM)
SINK

(TUN)
SWALLOW

(TOU)
SPIT

Types of Jook Wan Heun Ging Power

- **Look Ging Hop Yat - (6 Directional Powers):** This embodies the potential vector of directioal force the body can deploy power from. is part of every motion and refers to the motion of the force.
- **Sow Kai Boi - (Round the Back):** This is the power of Rounding and charging the Back with Potential kinetic power. The leverage piovts for this power are localized in the action of the Scapula gate girectly below the seventh cervical vertabre. The Mechanical action of this power is from the wrapping forward of the tendons and muscles. Parallel Aduction & Abduction power.

- **Gwun Ging - (Rolling Power):** This force is basically used when a bridge is involved. It rises while moving forward then drops. This power redirects oncoming force and crashes it, in a forward coiling motion.

- **Chum Ging: (Heavy Sinking power):** The achievement of this stage is the Iron body and unified combat frame.
- **Bik Ging:** Jamming forward power.
- **Jang Dai Lik Ging - (Elbow Sinking Power):** This is the power generated through the partnership of gravity and your intent to relax and sink with the elbow. The effect of gravities pull on the Elbow actes to not only stablizes the movement and Ging produced by the arm but also to unite the bodies frame over time.

- **Dip Gwat Ging - (Rib Bone Compression Power):** The power cultivated in the compression of the Rib bones, Latisimus muscles, Back (trapizious & scapula) etc. This element of movement contributes to the forward/backward element of "Lok Ging". This power cultivation also strengthens the bodies **Golden bell** aka **Iron Shirt**.
- **Sing Ging:** *(light, Floating and uprooting power).* This leaves the opponent feels that he can not root himself properly and that you provide not a hint of leverage for him. At this stage, you have full command of your body.

- **Jik Ging: (Direct Forward Explelling/discharging Power.)**
In Attacking one forges ahead never to back out. At The accomplishment of this stage techniques are clean and crisp. Extended tools never need to be retracted.
It charges on Ruthlessly & Relentlessly.

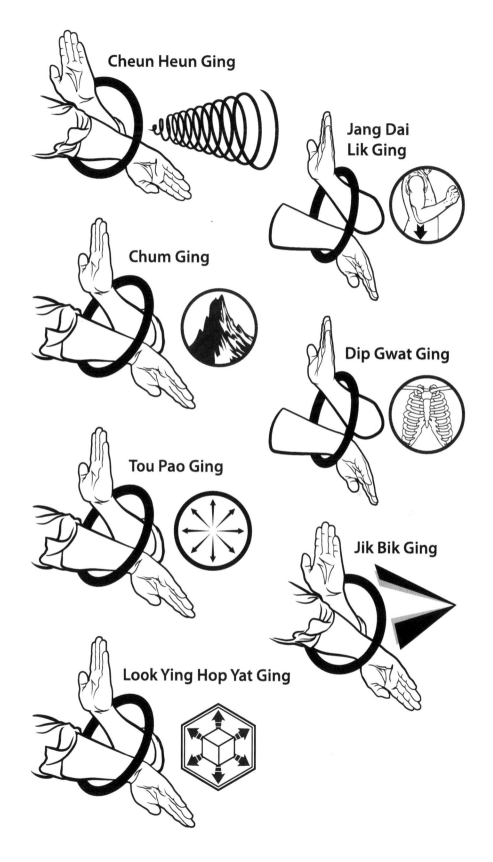

The Five Fundamental Pivots

When an Individual begins training in Wing Chun Kung Fu regardless of the branch, a student is first introduced too the basic structural detail for generating power. Those power details are first presented in the structure of the fundamental Wing Chun stance the Yee Gee Kim Yeung Ma (Character two goat clamping horse). This stance allows the practitioner to solidify and galvanize a rooted position of power and also develops a special Axis of rotation.

Now the concept of an Axis is crucial to the structural method of how power is generated which is through rotation, however that axis must be rooted with stability to effectively generate power. The first stage of this Axis and it's construction places it within the body running from the top of the head at a location called the **Pai Hui** *(Nine crowns gate)* point at the crown of the head. Extending down the length of the body through the pelvis ending at the **Doo Mai** *(Grain path)* point located between the genitals and anus. This Axis begins to make the practitioner more aware of gravities role in the partnership of stability necessary to begin building the foundation of successful Martial boxing.

Now this relationship to gravities pull is critical to maintain a rooted position of power but also begin uniting the kinetic springs of the body's skeletal frame to also discharge power to the attacker. There are three primary kinetic spring systems that discharge power from the body, they are **First** the stance, **Second** the Spine or core trunk mass and **Third** the Arm Sphere or the bridge arm wedge *(Som Kwok kiu).* Over time these three power spring systems unite and anchor themselves into the vertical mother Axis plane described previously.

Once the vertical mother Axis is stable that two dimensional plane evolves into a three dimensional plane with the integration of the three kinetic spring systems and causes the apex of this power plane to extend beyond the body. Over time with practice the practitioners ability to channel their full body mass through this plane toward an attack begins to transform into the ability the apply that force in an expanding or contracting sphere.

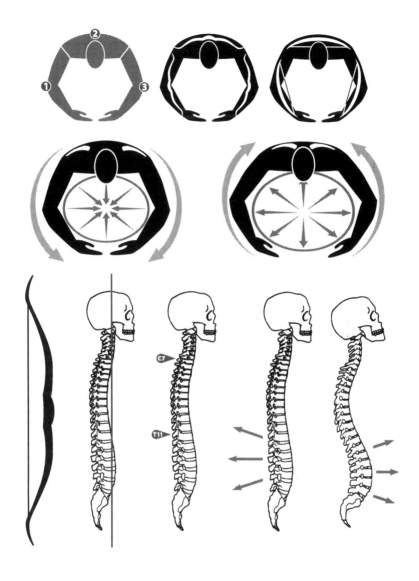

SOM KWOK KIU - TRIANGULAR DISPLACEMENT BRIDGE

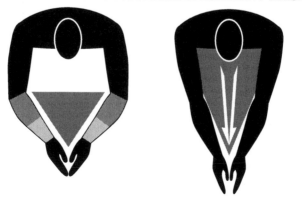

There is a fundamental cascade of principles that grow out of these structural relationships, one considered basic is the principle of gate theory or tactical spacial thresholds. Within most Martial traditions this principle of dividing the body plane and establishing bilateral symmetry is given the next dimension when the center gate mid line is established.

This is done by connecting the elbows with a line that runs through the solar plexus, now many reading this are already familiar with this structural detail however their is one related to this that is less well known but hidden in plane sight. The shadow line is a plane that wraps around the body even though the initial details are hidden behind the posture and position of **Lan sao** *(barring/retarding arm)*. The Shadow line or more bluntly the Nipple line is both a region that generates power based on position but also is one of four of the most dangerous target regions you must protect.

Jook wan training at it's core adds a level of ballistic rotation to all movements and techniques within Wing Chun Kung Fu. It is this heightened level of rotational, coiling movement (**Cheun ging**) that imparts added levels of power. During the initial stages of Jook wan training there are **5 fundamental points of pivot** rotation that the ring sets develop.

(1) Central pivot
The first pivot principle is called **Central pivot,** and just as it's name implies this point of rotation is at the exact center of the Jook wan ring. The central pivot concept takes the structural template of the Jook wan circle to teach the student to root this pivot axis with the core axis plane of their body and that of the Wing Chun stance.

The act of uniting the central pivot contained within the Jook wan to that of the stance creates a virtual axis that extends beyond the body and imparts an element of expansive and contractive movements not general focused of within some empty hand forms.
This first level helps the practitioner become more aware of a sensation of rotating expansion as they extend their arms along the center line plane. The Jook wan at this level also acts as a governing tool to keep the arms on a fixed orbit and fixed patrol route within the shoulder boundary lines.

5 Fundamental Pivots

⊙	Central Pivot	中心樞紐
⊖	Circumference Pivot	周長樞紐
⊚	Extended Pivot	延長樞紐
⊙)	Expansive Pivot	膨脹樞紐
⊕	Root Pivot	根樞紐

Fou - *Float*

Chum - *Sink*

Tun - *Swallow*

Tou - *Spit*

(2) Circumference Pivot

The second level of pivot mechanics is **Circumference Pivot**, this takes the central pivot and extends it to the circumference of the Jook wan. At this stage of practice the student is given a level of real time instantaneous tactile feed back, as rotational pressure from one bridge arm transmits pressure immediately to the other through the rings circumference.

This takes place in both the polarized and unpolarized ring positions and highlights the importance of keeping both arms in contact at all times with the innner circumference. The timing of each arms rotation and the calibration of that act is a focus of this level as well as the rooting of the elbows at important moments within movements transitions.

(3) Extended Pivot

The Third level of pivot mechanics is **Extended Pivot**, this takes one of the circumference pivots and anchors it so that the opposite pivot point on the circumference is allowed to extend beyond the circumference of the ring. This literally permits the practitioner to *"change gears"* and as when using a larger circumference with a lever and pulley system or the gears used in a bike, a greater load of both pressure from the attack can be dissolved and greater power discharged at the attacker.

This is a critical detail within the mechanics of any martial system, and that is, if the pivot point of rotation between two bodies exists at the center of the movement conflict then neither body will receive the combined momentum force produced. This is changed entirely if one of the two bodies adopts the same structural model of virtual axis rotation and diverts or discharges the force back at the other doing so with the fully combined momentum force.

A very crude and familiar example is that of a **Matador and Bull**. The **Matador** uses the decoy axis of *"The Cape"* to both distract and divert the momentum force of the **Bull**, but unlike the Matador and Bull example the stage of discharging attack force back at the attacker lies in the sudden contraction and implosion of the rotational circumference sphere in question.

CENTRAL PIVOT

中心樞紐

CIRCUMFERENCE PIVOT

周長樞紐

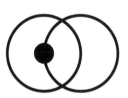

EXTENDED PIVOT

延長樞紐

EXPANSIVE PIVOT

膨脹樞紐

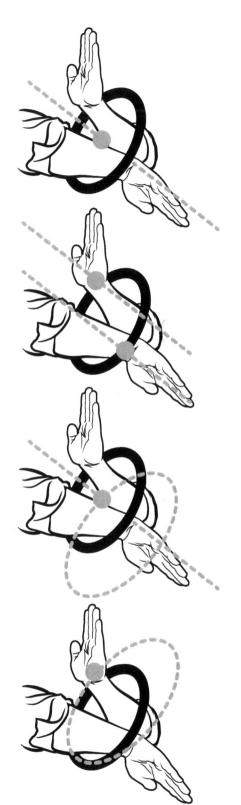

This base line of power is spiked through the roof if the practitioner in question who is discharging the force has all three kinetic spring systems unified. Each of the kinetic spring systems acts as a electrical transformer station to boost and amplify the Ging power, so that an individual weighing 120 pound can strike with the force of a 360 pound person. A simple formula example is that each kinetic spring systems, in our case 3 basic ones, collectively give the user three times the potential level of discharge power.

(4) Expansive Pivot
The Fourth level of Expansive pivot will vary according to the practitioner and focuses on the vertical axis that runs through the forearm and the tappering suface area on the outside.

If the outside surface area of the forearm has a greater tapper from elbow to wrist *(creating a conical shape)* then the potential level of coiled Inch power is increased. This is not only due to the inherent probability of greater and more developed muscular force but more accurately the ability based on shape to emit greater inch power based on ballistic tapered rotation.

An example meant to highlight this structural detail is that of a Wood screw verses a machine screw. First a **Machine screw** is like a cylinder in structure and has no tapper, and because there is no tapper such a structured shape cannot compact or accelerate the coil of rotation it manifests. However the structural shape of a **Wood screw** is by it's very shape designed to bore through a surface on contact requiring minimal forward pressure to facilitate deep penetration and thus manifests ballistic power.

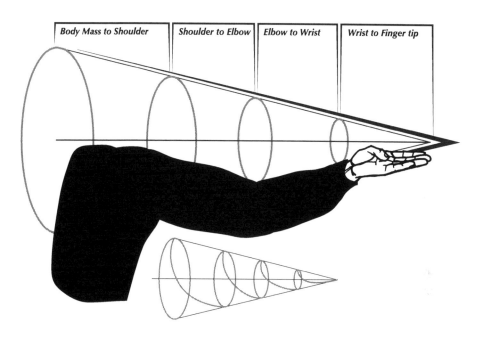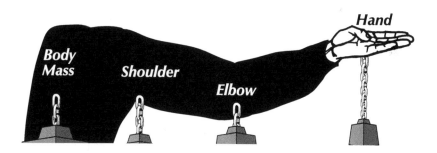

(5) Root Pivot

The Fifth level is Root pivot, and at this stage the term "Root" is meant to denote several ideas, the first of which is training without the ring at all. In much the same way as a practitioner spends time training on the Wooden dummy, and then steps away to perform what is called **Hei Jong/ Hong Mook yat jong fot** or *"Air Wooden dummy method"*.

Much like playing Air Guitar a practitioner is training the movements and techniques of the dummy without the structural corrective benefits of the dummy. Following this training theme a practitioner is putting the Jook wan aside and practising the movements of the ring and the structural details Jook wan training is meant to impart.

Training at the **Root stage** is meant to apply the pivots that have been developed, those that stick with the practitioner, and to move as if the ring were still there with an element of free flow application and interpretation. The next detail of practice has to due with how a plant sends down roots or more specifically root runners.
As bamboo grows it sends out in all directions smaller roots that act like feelers to establish root bases around it and propagate the plant. For the Jook wan practitioner it is the ability to manifest and apply multiple pivot point simultaneously within Wing Chun movements.

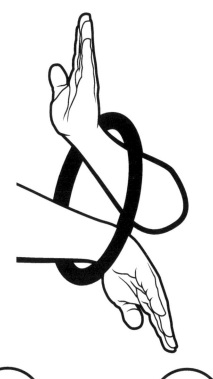

竹子圓詠春拳

Central Pivot
中心樞紐

Circumference Pivot
周長樞紐

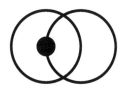

Extended Pivot
延長樞紐

Expansive Pivot
膨脹樞紐

Root Pivot
根樞紐

© Copyright 2013 Everything Wing Chun, LLC - All Rights reserved

Jook Wan Heun Martial Maxims

Sau Gay Loot Soong Syeung Moh Duck
Remain disciplined—conduct yourself ethically as a martial artist.

Ming Lai Yee Ngoy Goke Juen Chun
Practice courtesy and righteousness—serve the community and respect your elders.

Ngoy Toang Hock Tuen Geet Loke Kwun
Love your fellow students—be united and avoid conflicts.

Jeet Sick Yoke Boh Sau Jing Sun
Limit your desires and pursuit of bodily pleasures—preserve the proper spirit.

Kun Leen Jop Gay But Lay Sun
Train diligently—maintain your skills.

Hock Yeung Hay Gai Lum Dau Jung
Learn to develop spiritual tranquility—abstain from arguments and fights.

Syeung Chue Sai Tai Doh Wun Mun
Participate in society—be conservative and gentle in your manners.

Foo Yeuk Siu Yee Moh Foo Yun
Help the weak and the very young—use your martial skills for the good of humanity.

Gai Gwong Soy Hoan Gay Joh Fun
Pass on the tradition—preserve this Chinese art and its Rules of Conduct.

Gau Foong Yiu Han
You must be ferocious when clashing

Chuet Kuen Yiu Fai
The fist must be fast

Fot Lick Yiu Ging
Power must be used to release strength

See Gan Yiu Joon
Timing must be accurate

Fon Sau Yiu Leen
Trapping Hands must be continuous

Hay Lick Yiu Lau
Some of your strength must be kept in reserve

Ying Sai Yiu Sau
Your own posture must be protected

Ngon Sun Yiu Gau
Eye power and focus must be sharp

Yiu Ma Yiu Hup
The waist and stance must be united

Sau Gyeuk Yiu Ying
Hands and feet must be coordinated

Doang Joke Yiu Ling
Movements must be agile

Yum Yeung Yiu Sick
The principles of Yin and Yang must be comprehended

Sum Jing Yiu Ging
The spirit must remain calm

Hay Lick Yiu Ding
Breathing and strength must be steady

Loy Hay Yiu Chum
Internal strength must be sunken

Moh Sai Yiu Wai
The fighting demeanor must be commanding

Kuet Jeen Yiu Jook
A fight must end quickly

Tai Yeuk Lick Seen Sau Wai Jop But Hoh Lau
A weak body must start Do not keep any bad habits with strength improvement

- The shifting of a single pillar will shake all the beams, Attack the root of structure

- Best to bestow a single skill on a student than a thousand pieces of gold.

- Posses a single skill, and reap the benefits for a lifetime.

- Maintain your focus and you can bore through an army of ten thousand opponents.

- Boldness of execution stems from superb skill.

- In the area of learning, age makes no
Difference, those who know will always be the teacher of others.

- Study and Inquiry are the path to knowledge.

- One Mind, One Body, One Power.

- Strike first and prevail, Strike late and fail.

- Forced memorization is not as good as natural realization, this is an organic Martial awakening.

- Unity is Strength, - Structural Unity can turn dirt into Gold.

- If you chase after two rabbits, you'll catch neither. Focus on one attacker at a time.

- Those who fail to secure more than one Escape deserve to die.

- A clever Animal has three burrows, A clever Martial artist has three forms of Back-up or three forms of escape.

- When the time comes to apply knowledge, we always regret our lack thereof.

- A good quality of another may provide the remedy or solution for our own faults.

- You can't gain knowledge without practice, Wisdom comes from experience. Fall behind in practice and your skills will fade.

- Sand is minute, but it will harm your Eyes.
(Any attack is an Attack.)

- Those who bully the weak are cowards before the strong.

- If you strike someone with your fists, Beware of a kick in return.

- Diligence is a priceless treasure, and Caution is a talisman for survival.

- If you don't kill the Root the weed will return.

- When a Nest is overturned all eggs are broken, When the Attackers balance is broken all potential attacks are overturned.

- Try anything in a desperate situation.

- Two Attacks are one, and one attack is none. For the highest probability of successful striking deploy multiple attacks.

- Emphasize power, speed, accuracy, Balance, aggressiveness.

- The techniques are quickly chained.

- Seek to dominate straight from the outside top bridge contact reference.

- Seek to Turn & roll force from the inside bottom bridge contact reference.

- At first contact the attacker must fall of their horse (Off balance).

- The first Strike must make the attacker taste their spine. (Break the vertical structure support of the spine).

- Sink the Elbow to regain control.

- Use Shearing force to steer the attacker.

- Use Drilling force to drive the attacker.

- **Hum Hon** (Collapse & Swallow the chest).

- **Bat Boi** (Hunch back).

- **Chong Jao** (Tightly squeeze close the armpits).

- **An Dao Sao Dao** (The eyes and hands act together).

- *Yao Kiu Kiu Cern Gor -*
(If there is a bridge, then cross it.)

- *Mo Kiu Kiu Ha Cheun -*
(If there is no bridge, then make one.)

- *Yao Kiu Kiu Soi Kiu -*
(If there is a bridge, then Break it.)

- *Yao Kiu Kiu Gop Kiu -*
(If there is a bridge, then Trap it.)

- *Lurn Sao Bot Gwai Choi Sao Juen -*
(The hands don't draw back to extend forward.)

- Each movement must be packed into your Bone Marrow.

- Practice once a day, & you gain a Day. Skip a Day and you will loose ten days.

- Strive to remain calm in the midst of motion; loosen up the muscles and relax the mind.

- When entering, dominate the outside top Bridge reference, to control the situation.

- Do not collide with a strong opponent; with a weak opponent use a direct frontal assault.

- A quick fight should be ended quickly; no delay can be allowed.

- Iron fingers can strike a vital point at once.

- The stepping in elbow strike has sufficient threatening power.

- The phoenix eye punch has no equal.

- Springy power and the extended arm are applied to close range.

- Power starts from the heart and shoots towards the centerline.

- Power can be released in the intended manner; use of the line and position will be proper and hard to defeat.

- When facing multiple opponents, it is easy to manage the situation.

- When Wrist touch Wrist, A kick does not miss.

- The feet are like wheels, and the hands like arrows.

- A hand used for attack serves also to parry.

- Kicking to the head is like punching to the foot. Kicks lose nine times out of ten.

© Copyright 2013 Everything Wing Chun, LLC - All Rights reserved

WING CHUN TERMINOLOGY

Bak gek = sparring
Bai ying = losing body structure or loss of balance
Bai ying chi sau = irregular structure sticky hands
Bai ying jing ngau gurk = to regain lost balance by controlling with a front instep kick
Bai Ying ngoi au gurk = to regain lost balance by controlling with an inside instep kick
Bat jaam do = eight slash knives; the name of the Wing Chun butterfly knives and the knife form
Bat sin choi chi sau = 8 immortal table sticky hands for demonstrations
Bau ja geng = whipping or explode energy
Bau ja lik = explode power
Bik bo = jamming stance in the knive form
Bik ma = chasing stance with the pole
Bo lay ying = glass technique
Bok = shoulder
Bong an chi sau = blindfolded sticky hands
Bong do = wing arm block with the butterfly knives
Bong family = a family of Wing Chun techniques that contact on the little finger side of the wrist
Bong gurk = outer shin bock with the knee turned outward
Bong sau = wing arm block contacting on the wrist area
Biu do = shooting or thrusting with the knives also the stance to step forward
Biu gee = shooting fingers
Biu gee ma / Cao Bo = outward circling stance
Biu gwan or Biu kwan = shooting or thrusting with the pole
Biu jong sau = centerline thrusting block or strike with the thumb side up, contacting on the thumb side of the wrist
Biu ma = shooting forward stance with the pole
Biu sau = shooting fingers block, contacting on the little finger side of the wrist
Chum = to sink, one of the principles of the Siu Lum Tau
Chum geng = sinking power to duck away from attacks
Chum bo = go forward and jam stance in the knive form
Chum do = a upper slash or chop with the butterfly knives
Chum jeong = to "push out" with the palm; an upper gate palm strike that drills

out with the palm
Chop kuen = low punch
Chai gurk = any kick that stamps down; also a scraping kick contacting with the
blade edge of the foot
Chai sut = to stomp downward with the knee
Chair kuen = pulling punch; the Wing Chun basic rotational punch
Chan dai jeorng or dai chan jeorng also juk jeong = to "cut in"; a low knife edge palm
strike, contacting with the little finger side and with the palm up
Chang gang = neck chop with the little finger side of the palm down or palm up
Chang jeong = "knife edge" palm strike contacting with the little finger side of the palm
Cheeng chong ma or jing chor ma = forward bracing stance
Chi = 1) internal energy 2) sticking
Dan chi gurk = single sticky legs exercise
Chi do = sticky knives
Chi gok chi sau or ji gok chi sau = light sticky hands
Chi geng = sticking energy
Chi gung = internal energy exercises
Chi gurk = sticky legs exercise
Chi gwan or chi kwan = sticky pole exercise
Chi sau = sticky hands exercises; there are many types of chi sau
Chi sau chi gurk = sticky hands and legs exercise
Chi seurng gurk or chi gurk = double sticky legs exercise
Chi sun = body sticking
Choi geng = taking over power
Choeng kui jeong = long bridge palm that drills as the stance turns, contacting
with the little finger side of the palm; from the Bue Gee form
Choeng kiu lik = long bridge power
Chong jou si gan = creating timing
Chuen ma or Chor ma = "sitting" horse stance, the basic turning stance
Chor do or Ding do = stomping with the knife handle
Chou gurk or Dim gurk = snapping front kick
Choung chi = aggressive energy
Choung geng = forward, aggressive power
Chour kuen or chour tau kuen = hammerfist

Chui meen joi ying = follow the structure; straight on facing and chasing
Chui ying = facing straight-on structure; facing the shadow
Chum bo = cat sinking stance in the knife form
Chum jarng = sinking elbow bock; immovable elbow line
Chum Kiu = 1) searching for the bridge 2) the name of the second form, sinking the bridge
Chum sun = to evade by sinking the body, ducking
Chun geng or Duan geng = short thrusting power
Chun geng kuen = one inch punch, a short punch
Chuun lop = moving stancework between the poles in the mui fa jong
Chung kiu lik = long bridge power
Chung kuen or Jik kuen or Yat chi chung kuen = straight punch
Churng wai = stealing the line
Churng wai chi sau = stealing the line or regaining the line in chi sau
Da = a strike or hit
Da m' Jarn or Wu Jarn = 5 elbows exercise
Tai Jarn = raising elbow
Gwai Jarn or Cup Jarn = diagonal downward elbow
Wang Jarn = outward horizontal elbow
Pai Jarn = inward horizontal elbow
Hau Jarn = retracting or rear elbow
Daai geng = directing energy
Dai = low or lower level attack
Dai bong sau or dai pong sau = low level wing arm block
Dai chan jeong or Chang Dai Jueng = low knife edge palm strike
Dai Lim Tau = big idea which is built up from the little ideas in the Siu Lim Tau form
Dai gurk = low kick
Dai au gurk = low roundhouse
Dai jing gurk = low front kick
Dai wang gurk = low side kick
Dai jeong or haa jeong = low level spade thrust palm strike
Dan chi sau = single sticky hands exercise
Dan tien = the center of energy in the body located about two inches below
the navel in center of the trunk
Dang gurk = nailing kick
Dang gwan or dang kwan = snapping straight down with the pole

Day har au gurk = roundhouse kick on the floor
Day har chi gurk = sticky legs on the floor
Day har jing gurk = front kick on the floor
Day har wang gurk = side kick on the floor
Day ton bok gek = ground fighting
Deng or tai gurk = raising kick
Dim gwan or dim kwan =stabbing pole
Dim ma = stamping in the pole stance to give more energy
Ding sau = bent wrist block or strike contacting with the wrist area
Dit da = injuries such as bruises, sprains and strains
Dit da jau or dit da jow = herbal liniment for bruises, sprains, and strains
Doi gok gurk = low diagonal leg block or strike
Doi gok kuen or wang kuen or Oi gok kuen = diagonal punch from
outside across the centerline
Dok gurk or Dok lop ma - Siu Lim Tau = single leg form of Siu Lim Ta
Do = butterfly knives
Do bo = moving stances with the knives
Duun or Duan geng = short inches power
Faan dan chi sau = bouncing sticky hands
Faan sau = continuous lop sau basic attack to break through the opponent's structure
Faan kuen = circling punch either inside or outside
Hoi faan kuen or Oyi faan kuen = outside whip punch
Ngoi faan kuen = inside whip punch
Faan kuen or faan sau = continuous attacking with controlling while alternating punches as in
pak faan sau, bue faan sau and lop faan sau
Faan sun = to regain the body position
Faan sun jing gurk = to regain the body position with a front kick
Fak do = upward deflecting block with the knives
Fak sau = upward deflecting block swinging the forearm down and up,
contacting with the little finger side of the wrist.
Fat do = right power in techniques
Faun au gurk or fong ngau gurk = reverse roundhouse
Fay jong or Fai jarn = flying elbows
Fong sau sin wai = blocking line

Fook family = a family of Wing Chun techniques which use the palm
Fook gurk = a downward leg block or strike contacting with the muscle next to the shin bone
Fook sau = a palm controlling block with the elbow down
Fook sut = an inward knee block or strike
Fong sau sin wai = blocking line
Fung ngan kuen or fung an kuen = phoenix eye punch with the index knuckle forward
Fuun do = an outward or sidewards slash with the butterfly knives
Fuun sau = an outward or sidewards horizontal chop
Ga chok = bouncing technique off of an opponent's structure
Gan jip geng = indirect or clining power
Gaan da = simultaneous low sweeping block with a punch
Gaan gurk = 3 leg blocking exercise with the following blocks:
Dai jing gurk = low front kick blocking with the calf muscle
Bong gurk = shin block
Gut gurk = snapping block
Gaan jaam = simultaneous low sweeping block with a forearm deflecting block or chop.
Gaan jaam do = simultaneous low sweeping bock and upper deflecting
block with the butterfly knives.
Gaan sau = a low sweeping block. There are two kinds of gaan sau
Noi gaan sau = an outward low sweeping block
Ngoi gaan sau = an inward low sweeping block
Gaan sau = 5 blocking motions
Ngoi gaan sau = inside low sweeping block
Tan sau = flat palm-up block contacting on the thumb side of the wrist
Noi gaan sau = outside low sweeping block
Jam sau = forearm deflecting block
Wu sau = guard hand block
Gee = fingers
Gee gok chi sau or ji or chi gok chi sau = light sticky hands
Gee gok geng or gum gok geng = feeling power
Geng or ging = energy; the 8 types of Wing Chun energy are:
  1. BAU JA GENG = EXPLODE POWER
  2. CHI GENG = STICKING POWER
  3. KENG GENG = LISTENING POWER
  4. JUUN GENG = DRILLING POWER

* 5. JEK JIP GENG = DIRECT POWER
* Gan jip geng = indirect power
* 6. YAAN GENG OR DAAI GENG = GUIDING POWER
* 7. LIN JIP GENG = CONNECTING POWER
* 8. CHOUNG GENG = AGGRESSIVE POWER

Gin kuen = moving side punch for pole exercise
Goiu ying = adjusting the body structure
Goot do = cutting knife attack
Goot gwan = cutting down with the pole
Gor dan chi sau = attacks in single sticky hands
Gor lop sau = attacks in lop sau
Gor sau or guo sau = attacks in sticky hands
Gour yung = guts or determination and self-confidence to win
Gu deng chi sau = sitting sticky hands
Gum gok geng, gee gok geng or ji gok geng = feeling energy
Gum jeong = low palm edge strike
Gum sau = downward palm block or strike with the elbow turned outward
Gum ying = body feeling
Gung gek sin wai = attacking line
Gung lik chi sau = heavy sticky hands to develop power
Gurk = leg or kick The 8 positions of the kick are
* 1. jing gurk = strike with the top of the heel just below the arch
* 2. wang gurk = strike with the outside of the heel on the little toe side
* 3. soo gurk = strike with the inside of the arch
* 4. yaai sut gurk = strike with the middle of the heel downward
* 5. tiu gurk = strike with the instep with the toes pointed
* 6. jut gurk = strike with the lower calf and achilles tendon
* 7. tai sut = strike with the top or side of the knee with the leg bent
* 8. chai gurk = strike downward with the knife edge of the foot

Gurk jong = 8 kicks to the mok jong or dummy
Gurng gee kuen or Ger nah choi = ginger fist punch
Gwai jarng or Cup jarng = a circular downward elbow block or strike
contacting with the forearm.
Gwai sut = a downward knee block contacting with the side of the knee or shin
Gwan or kwan = pole
Gwang geng = steel-bar power
Gwat ji fat lik = bone-joint power

Gwat gwan or sut gwan = opening up or blocking the inside or outside lower gate with the pole
Gwat sau = a circular controlling technique that carries the subject
across the centerline to open an attacking line.
Haa or chaap kuen = low punch
Haa jeong or dai jeong = low palm strike with the side of the palm
Haan = economic motion
Haan kiu = walking on the bridge or forearm
Haan kiu chi sau = walking on the bridge chi sau
Haan sau = a long bridge block contacting with the little finger side of the wrist
Hau chong ma = backward bracing stance
Hau huen joon ma or hau huen or hau joon =- a turning stance that is executed by stepping
forward then turning 180 degrees to face the opposite direction
Hau jeong = a palm strike with the back of the palm
Hay jarng or Tai jarng = raising elbow strike or block
Hay sau or tai sau or ding sau = a raising bent wrist block or strike contacting
on the little finger side of the wrist
Hay sut or tai sut = raising knee block or strike contacting with the top or side of the knee
Ho Kam Ming = a long time disciple of Grandmaster Yip Man; the teacher
of Augustine Fong (Fong Chi-Wing)
Hoi or oi =outside
Hoi bok = outside shoulder
Hoi faan kuen = outside whip punch
Hoi hurn = outside facing stance
Hoi jeorng or hau jerong = back palm strike or block
Hoi jung sin = outside line
Hoi kwan sau = outside rolling hands block
Hoi ma = to open the horse stance
Hoi moon chi sau or hoi mun chi sau = outside gate (position) chi sau
Hoi moon kuen or hoi mun kuen = outside gate diagonal punch
Hoi sik = opening position
Hoiu = emptiness, one of the major principles of Siu Lim Tau
Hoiu bo = empty step or cat stance in the pole form

Hoiu ying = empty shadow
Huen da = simultaneous circling with one hand and striking with the other
Huen fok sau = circling one hand into the fok sau position
Huen gurk = any circle kick
Huen jing gurk = circling front kick
Huen wang gurk = circling side kick
Huen tiu gurk = circling instep kick
Huen ma = circling stance in the pole form
Huen sau = circling, controlling hand
Huiu ma = cat stance in the pole form
Hung jai = control of power
Hung jai chi sau = controlling sticky hands motion to block the opponent
Hung jai geng = controlling energy
Jam jong = stance for chi gung
Jaam do = a forward deflecting block with the butterfly knives
Jaam sau = a forearm deflecting block contacting with the little finger side of the forearm
hoi jaam sau = outside wu sau
ngoi jaam sau= inside jaam sau
Jau ma or jou ma = combining moving footwork
Jau mui fa jong = stancework on the plum blossom
Jau sau = changing lines in attacks, going from one line to another
Jau wai = moving stances while changing from one line to another
Jau wai chi sau or ngou sau = moving sticky hands while changing lines
Jau wai yaai sut = moving stances to attack with the knees
Jek jip geng = direct power
Jeong = palm strike or chop; the 8 palm strikes are
* 1. jing jeong = front vertical palm
* 2. choen kui jeong = long bridge palm
* 3. hau jeong = back palm
* 4. dai jeong = low side palm
* 5. pau jeong = downward vertical palm strike
* 6. gum sau = diagonally downward palm strike
* 7. chan jeong = knife edge palm strike to upper body and head with palm up
* 8. wang jeong = side of palm strike to upper body and head with palm down
Ji gok chi sau, gee or chi gok chi sau = light sticky hands
Ji yau bak gek = free sparring

Jing = front or center
Jing = quietness; one of the major principles of the Siu Lim Tau form
Jing bok = front shoulder
Jing chor ma or cheen chor ma = forward bracing stance
Jing dok lop ma or jing gurk dok lop ma = front single leg stance
Jing gurk = front kick
Jing jeorng = straight vertical palm strike
Jing jung = any strike on the center
Jing ma or yee gee kim yeung ma = front developmental stance; it is not a stance to fight from
Jing meen = facing to the front
Jing ngour gurk = toe up hooking kick or control
Jing sun = Wing Chun front-on body structure
Jin kuen = punches from the pole horse stance
Jit gurk = stopping a kick with a kick
Jip sau = "controlling the bridge"; an arm break
Joi geng = chasing power
Joi yin = following the shadow
Joi yin chi sau = following the shadow in chi sau; a type of chasing chi sau
Joi yin jong = folowing the shadow on the floor
Jon geng or juun geng = drilling power
Jong = elbow
Jong dai lik = elbow power produced from practicing the punch
Jong gek or Bik jarng = elbow pushing from behind
Jong sau = 1) a centerline block or strike contacting with the thumb side of the wrist
2) the general name for the Wing Chun fighting position
Joong-lo = mid-level
Joong-lo kuen = mid-section drilling punch
Juen ma = turning and circling stance with the pole
Juk dok lop ma or wang dok lop ma = side single leg stance
Jung sin = centerline or centerline plane
ngoi jung sin = inside line
hoi jung sin = outside line
Jung sum sin = vertical motherline
Juun geng = drilling power
Jut = snapping motion
Jut da = simultaneous snapping control with one hand and striking with the other
Jut do = snapping the knives sideways

Jut geng = snapping power
Jut gurk = snapping kick or block
Jut sau = snapping block contacting with the thumb side of the wrist
Kau sau or kow sau = hooking palm control
Keng geng = listening power
Kit gwan or kit kwan = opening up or blocking the inside, upper gate with the pole
Kuen = fist or punch
8 families of Wing Chun punches are:
* 1. yat chi chung kuen = pulling vertical punch
* 2. chaap kuen = low punch
* 3. ngoi faan kuen = inside whip punch
* 4. hoi faan kuen = outside whip punch
* 5. oi gok kuen = diagonal punch
* 6. chour kuen = hammerfist
* 7. joong-lo kuen = drilling punch
* 8. tai kuen = raising punch
Kuen siu kuen = punch to punch exercise
Kuen to = any hand form
Kiu = bridge or forearm
Kiu li = distance to the bridge
Kiu sau = arm bridge
Kum la = joint locking techniques
Kum la chi sau = joint locking techniques applied in chi sau
Kwak sau = double spreading huen sau
Kwan or gwan = pole
Kwan = rolling
Kwan do = rolling knives
Kwan ma = pole stance
Kwan sau = rolling hands block
La ma = the stable, rooting stance in the pole form
Lan gwan or lan kwan = horizontal long bridge pole
Lan gurk = horizontal leg block contacting with the shin bone
Lan sau = horizontal arm block contacting with forearm and sometimes palm
Lau do = twisting the knives inward to block and strike
Lay wai chi sau = leaving the gap sticky hands
Lik = muscular strength
Lik do = the correct power
Lin jip geng = connecting power or energy

Lin siu dai da = economy of motion
Lin wan kuen = continuous chain punching
Ling gung jau = muscle liniment
Lin wai gurk = flowing kicks
Look sau or luk sau or gung lik chi sau = heavy sticky hands
Lop = grabbing or controlling with the palm
Lop da = simultanteous controlling and striking ; also refers to a partner exercise
Lop chan jeong = simultaneous palm controlling and heel palm strike
Lop fook = grabbing from fook sau position
Lop sau = grabbing hand control; also refers to a partner exercise
Lop sau chi sau = lop sau in sticky hands
Lou gwan or low gwan = the half point pole technique; a short thrust
Luk dim bune gwan or luk dim boon gwan = six and half point pole form
Lut sau = attacking without initial contact with the opponent's bridge; it begins with fighting position
Lut sau chi sau = attacking from man sau position and immediately going into sticky hands
Ma = stance
Ma bo = moving stances
Ma bo chi sau = moving sticky hands
Ma bo lop sau = moving lop sau
Mai jong = the correct elbow position with the elbow inward on the elbow line
Mai jong = closing the gap
Man = "to ask"
Man gurk = asking legs where the first motion sets up the second attack
Man sau = asking hands where the first motions sets up the second attack
Man sau chi sau = asking hand within sticky hands
Mo kiu chi sau = walking on the bridge sticky hands
Mo see = traditional lion dance
Mok lik = eye power with emotion
Mok jong or Mok yan jong = wooden dummy also the name for the wooden dummy form
Moon or mun = gate or door
say-i moon = dead gate which is closed

soung moon = live gate which is open
Mui fa jong = plum blossom posts and the name for the exercise of practicing on the posts
Ng Mui = the Buddhist Siu Lum nun who founded Wing Chun
Ng'an geng or ng'on geng= elastic power
Ngoi = inside
Ngoi bok = inside shoulder
Ngoi faan kuen = inside whip punch
Ngoi geng = internal power
Ngoi gung = internal chi exercises for fighting applications
Ngoi hurn = inside facing stance
Ngoi jung sin = inside line
Ngoi kwan sau = inside rolling hands
Ngoi moon kuen = inside gate diagonal punch
Ngoi moon chi sau = inside gate (position) chi sau
Ngoi ngau gurk = inside leg hook
Ng'on geng or ng'an geng = elastic power
Ngou sau = pushing and drilling while moving in chi sau
Oi or hoi = an alternative spelling for "outside"
Pai jarng = horizontal inward elbow strike
Pak da = simultaneous pushing palm block and punch
Pak do = catching knives block
Pak gurk = inside kick with the sole of the foot with the knee bent
Pak sau = pushing palm block or strike
Pak sut = inward knee block or strike
Pau jeong = flat palm strike with the fingers pointing down. This is applied to the lower body
Pau sau = lifting palm block
Ping haan geng = balancing or equalizing power
Ping sun = side turning body structure or position; this is not a Wing Chun position
Por jung = all techniques that control and "break" the centerline
Por si gan = breaking timing
Po bai or po pai = double butterfly palm strike
Poon sau = regular sticky hand motion
Pun doon = determination in a fight
Sa bau = the wall bag
Sam gung ma, Sam kwak ma or sip ma = 3 angle stance
San sau = slow attack exercise
San sau chi sau = slow attacks in sticky hands
Sat gwan = opening the lower gate to inside or outside with the

pole
Say bo or Toy ma = retreat and step back stance to deflect in the knife form
Say ping ma = low horse stance for pole
Say-i kuen = shooting punch
Say-i moon = dead gate
Sau = hand or arm
Sau gwan = retreating the pole
Sau jong = retracting elbow strike or block
Sau sik or sau sic = closing position in the forms
Sau wuun geng = equalizing the point and power; wrist power
Seng yum geng = sound power to emotionally trap an opponent
Seung = double (Two) or advancing
Seung bok = shoulder attacks
Seung chi sau = double sticky hands exercise
Seung dai bong = double low forearm block
Seung heun sau = double circling block
Seung jut sau = double snapping block
Seung kuen = double punch
Seung ma = front advancing stance
Seung pau sau = double upward palm block
Seung yan chi sau = double sticky hands with three people
Seung yan dan chi sau = single sticky hands with three people
Seung yan jou wai chi sau = moving sticky hands with three people
Seung yan lop sau = lop sau with three people
Seung yan man sau = man sau with three people
Seung tan sau = double palm up block
Si Bok = your teacher's Si-Hing
Si Dai = a male classmate who joined a school after you
Si Fu = your teacher can be either male or female
Si gan = timing
* 1. si gan sing = regular
* 2. tor chi si gan = delayed
* 3. por si gan = breaking
* 4. chong jou si gan = creating
* Si gan sing = regular timing
Si gan pui hop = the correct timing and power
Si Gung = your teacher's teacher
Si Hing = a male classmate who joined the school before you
Si Jay - a female classmate who joined the school before you

Si Jo = an ancestor within the system
Si ma = deflecting stance that braces the pole
Si Mo = your teacher's wife
Si Sook or si suk = your teacher's classmates who started after him
Sin = line
jung sin = centerline
ngoi jung sin = inside line
hoi jung sin = outside line
gung gek sin wai = attacking line
fong sau sin wai = blocking line
jung sum sin = vertical motherline
wang jung sin = horizontal motherline
Sing geng= raising power to destroy the opponent's structure
Sip ma, Sam Kwak ma or Sam gung ma = 3 angle stance
Siu geng = dissolving power
Siu Nim Tau = "small idea form" the first wing chun form
Soang jarng or wang jarng = outward horizontal elbow
Soo gurk = sweeping kick
Soor jung = sinking elbow down to control the centerline so the opponent cannot move you
Sor sau or Fon sau chi sau = trapping sticky hands
Soung moon = live gate
Sum gwang = 3 joints in the arm equivalent to the 3 gates to pass
Sun ying = body structure
Sup ji sau or sup gee sau = crossed arm block in all hand forms
Sut = knee
Taan gwan = snapping the pole sideways
Tai = raising or lifting
Tai gurk = raising kick
Tai gwan = raising pole
Tai jarng or hay jarng = raising elbow
Tai kuen = raising punch
Tai or dang sut = raising knee block or attack
Tak gurk = low instep kick
Tan da = simultaneous palm up block and punch
Tan da gaan da = simultanteous blocking and attacking exercise
Tan do = locking knife block
Tan geng ="swallowing" or sucking power to duck or control attacks
Tan gurk = forward and upward leg block
Tan ma = drawing back stance from horse or cat in the pole

Tan sau = palm up block contacting on the thumb side of the wrist
Tan sut = outward knee block or attack
Tang geng = a rubber- band like power
Teut sau or tuit sau = freeing arm block
Tit kiu sau = iron bridge
Tik gwan = opening the upper gate with the pole
Tiu do = snapping up knife
Tiu gwan or tiu kwan = snapping up pole
Tiu or tio gurk = jumping kick
Tiu gurk = instep kick
To gwan or to kwan = going forward with the pole
Toi dit = take downs
Toi dit chi sau = takedowns in chi sau
Toi ma = step back and turn stance
Tok sau or pau sau = lifting palm block
Tong do = slicing knife attack
Tor chi si gan = delayed timing
Toh ma or Tor ma = step slide stance
Tou geng= power that "spits out" or bounces the opponent away
Tou ma = advancing forward stance in the pole
Tui ma = jumping stance
Tun gwan or tun kwan = retracting pole
Tung ma = retreating jumping stance in the pole form
Wai ji = a good position
Wan bo = crossing step stance in the knife form
Wan do = circling knife attack
Wan ma = step and circle into other stances in the pole
Wang or wan = side
Wang gurk = side kick
Wang gurk dok lop ma = side kick single leg stance
Wang jeong or Ju jeong = side of palm strike with the palm down
Wang jong or pai jong = inside horizontal elbow
Wang jung sin = horizontal motherline
Wing Chun Tong = Wing Chun school
Won or huen gwan /kwan = following circle with the pole
Woot ma = flexible pole stance
Wu do = a strike with the knife hand guard
Wu gurk = blade edge of the foot block or strike
Wu sau = guard hand block contacting with the little finger side of the wrist
Wu yi sun - to return the body to a normal position

Wu yi ying = to regain the body structure
Wu yi ying bong sau = to regain the body structure with bong sau
Wu yi ying gum sau = to regain the body structure with gum sau
Wun geng, ngon geng, jut geng = jerking power
Yaai = to attack stepping down
Yaai hau gurk = to attack by stepping down on the opponent's rear leg
Yaai sut = to attack down with the knee
Yaan geng or daai geng = guiding power
Yang = everything that is strong, light, active male, etc.
Yang chi = the energy you inhale from air; oxygen
Yap jung lou = closing the gap
Yau = to relax; an essential principle of the Siu Lim Tau form
Yee gee kim yeung ma = the mother of all stances; the stationary front stance for developing all
stances which means two knees going in stance
Yee ma = transitions between the stances in the pole
Yee ying bo sau = using your structure to recover your position
Yim Wing Chun = the young lady that Ng Mui taught the Wing Chun system to. She further
refined and improved the system so it is named after her.
Yin = everything that is weak, dark, quiet, female, etc.
Yin and yang = a pair of opposites that constantly change. All things have both yin and yang and
all things change
Yin chi = energy you exhale or carbon dioxide
Ying = structure
Yip Man = the late grandmaster of Wing Chun who taught publically which spread the system
Yon geng = elastic power
Yuen geng = patience energy also the ability to make the opponent move they way you want
Yut bo = turning around stance in the knife form with fak do and also going through the legs
with the knives
Yut ge chon kuen or doi kou kuen or Yet chi chung kuen = vertical punch

Jook Wan Applications, All photo sequences follow a single downward vertical column and flow from top to bottom.
▼

Jook Wan Application - 1

Jook Wan Application - 2

Jook Wan Application - 3   # Jook Wan Application - 4

Jook Wan Application - 5

Jook Wan Application - 6

Jook Wan Application - 7

Jook Wan Application - 8

Jook Wan Application - 9

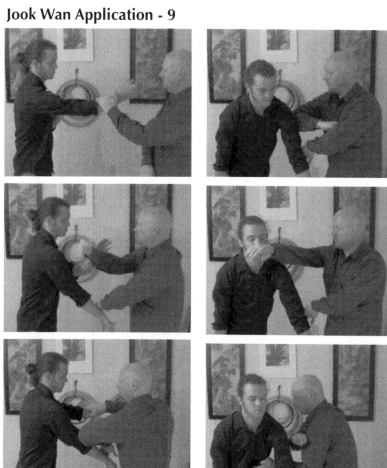

Jook Wan Application - 10

Jook Wan Application - 11

Jook Wan Application - 12

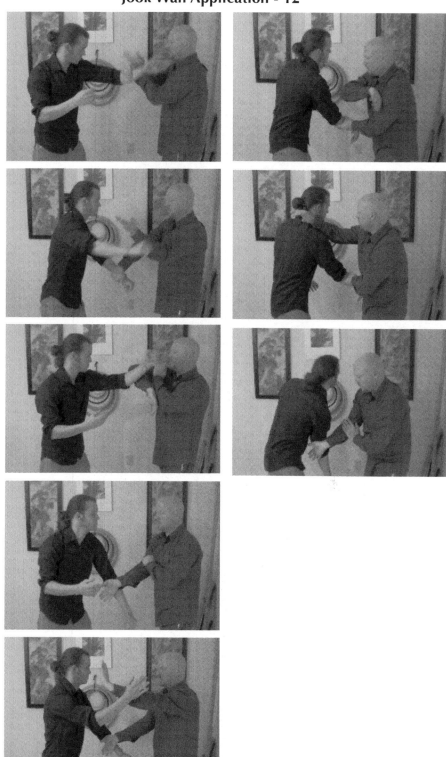

Jook Wan Application - 13

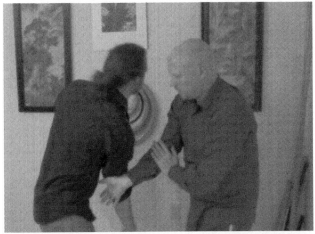

Jook Wan Application - 14

Jook Wan Application - 15

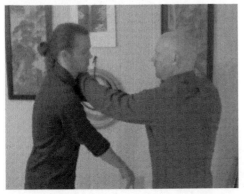

Jook Wan Application - 16

Jook Wan Application - 17

Jook Wan Application - 18

For more information
on the training of the
Jook Wan Heun
of Wing Chun Kung Fu
contact:

Sifu Tyler Rea
trea1701@gmail.com

Sifu Aaron Cantrell
Everything Wing Chun
www.everythingwingchun.com

Wing Chun University
www.wingchununiversity.com

© **Copyright 2013**
- **All Rights reserved -**

Made in the USA
Lexington, KY
10 October 2017